Arnold James Cooley

Two Months in a London Hospital

Its inner Life and Scenes

Arnold James Cooley

Two Months in a London Hospital
Its inner Life and Scenes

ISBN/EAN: 9783337243128

Printed in Europe, USA, Canada, Australia, Japan

Cover: Foto ©ninafisch / pixelio.de

More available books at **www.hansebooks.com**

TWO MONTHS

IN A

LONDON HOSPITAL.

TWO MONTHS

IN A

LONDON HOSPITAL;

ITS INNER LIFE AND SCENES.

A PERSONAL NARRATIVE,

BY

ARNOLD J. COOLEY,

Author of "*Cyclopædia of Receipts, Processes, Data, and Collateral Information,*"
"*Dictionary of the English Language,*" "*Latin Grammar,*"
&c., &c.

LONDON:
GROOMBRIDGE & SONS, 5, PATERNOSTER ROW.
—
MDCCCLXV.

LONDON:
J. E. ADLARD, PRINTER, BARTHOLOMEW CLOSE.

PREFACE.

THE origin of this little work is noticed in its introductory chapter. The fact of its having been produced, and subsequently arranged for the press, during my convalescence, will account for the desultory way in which the subject is treated. Were I at the present time, with the same materials at my command, to sit down to write a similar narrative, I should probably arrange and treat the subject differently; but I doubt whether the resulting work would possess equal interest to the present one. The advantages of orderly arrangement and precision possessed by the one, would be more than counterbalanced by the freshness, familiar style, and diversified character of the other. Besides this, many of the scenes, details, and remarks, crowded into the following pages, and which, I trust, will prove new and interesting to the majority of my readers, could not have been well introduced into a formal written narrative.

This work contains a "plain, unvarnished tale" of real life, in which no extrinsic aids have been called in to impart to it additional interest. I have concealed nothing, and have spoken freely and unreservedly on every subject that has come before me. I have been rigidly careful to admit nothing into its pages which, to the best of my knowledge and belief, is not strictly true. My desire throughout has been neither to flatter nor censure any person, or any thing, and to confine myself, as much as possible, to the details of my own case, and to what occurred immediately around me, with such additional matter only as I thought was necessary to interest the reader and render him familiar with hospital-life. If any thing which I have written bears an opposite construction, it is contrary to my intentions and wishes.

The *foot-notes* are later additions to the work, being added, with one or two exceptions, either immediately before or during its passage through the press.

As this work is intended to form a popular volume, I have scrupulously avoided the introduction of any thing into it of an abstruse, technical, or controversial character. The few technical terms which have been unavoidably used are explained in the foot-notes. For the same reason I have not entered at length into the subject of the 'Medical Schools' attached to our larger hospitals, nor the 'students' life there,' as not being immediately connected with the patients and the task I had undertaken. I trust, however, that notwithstanding its popular form, the professional reader will find many things in its pages that will interest him, and a few that are, perhaps, new to him.

In reference to the contents of Chapters VII.-X, I think it right to mention, that I do not hold myself responsible for the remarks and opinions expressed by me at the period to which these chapters refer. Undoubtedly, however, they took their peculiar tone from opinions I had held during some years of my previous life. I had long been impressed with the conviction that England is a Christian country *only* in name. I had long regarded much of our vaunted civilisation, religion, morality, and benevolence, as "like unto whited sepulchres, which indeed appear beautiful outward, but are within full of dead men's bones, and of all uncleanness," "full of hypocrisy and iniquity," and selfishness. Beyond the vast advances of the present age in physical science, chemistry, and civil engineering, and in civil and religious liberty, I fear it has little to boast of at the expense of the previous one. And even here, much of this apparent progress in England depends on our increased wealth, on increased facilities afforded by the legislature to great undertakings, and on the influence of a bold and independent press. There is *some* truth in the following remarks culled from a recent 'editorial' in a leading daily journal :—

"We are rather proud of the nineteenth century; we flatter ourselves that the twentieth will be hard pushed to beat it. We are rich, we are prosperous, we are strong; the poets ought to sit, we think, in gilded cages, and whistle 'songs without words' to us, to amuse, and not to bother. But the poets—the true ones—will not accept the part of singing birds; their strains are sad; they pipe condemnation at us; they chirrup contempt; their notes are full of melancholy and complaint, of shame and disgust, at an epoch which is almost wholly plunged in the base philosophies of the 'comfortable.' Look at us in our foreign relations: we are so fat and happy, and full of beef and wine, that as a people we only grunt displeasure when justice is trampled under foot. * * * John Bull runs all to belly, amid the sneers and scorn of Europe, and the despair of those who looked to him as the friend of liberty. At home it is the same; the pendulum of national life has swung down to the bottom of the arc. We amass wealth —we live upon the principles of Epicurus—we have got rid of religion, chivalry, enthusiasm, and principles; big houses, fine carriages, costly dinners, silks, velvets, and diamonds, are the grand pursuits of life. Chastity, simplicity, sincerity, and self-sacrifice, are things we read about, but see not. Modern chastity sometimes pays off its mistress when it marries; modern simplicity lisps out blasphemies at the clubs; modern sincerity runs a race-horse to lose a race; and modern self-sacrifice means sacrificing everything for self. The great golden stye wherein we all roll is quite in turmoil when its propriety is questioned, or when the signs of a sublime awakening of the common soul whisper that miracles are not past, nor religion a thing of Articles and outward forms, nor God annihilated, nor His world a thing created for eating and drinking, for the multiplying of shares and Sydenham villas. * * * * * Our painters are busy depicting 'railway stations' and 'life at the seaside,' and little girls sleeping through 'my second sermon;' our sculptors make a very good thing out of busts, and the ostentatiously nude, miscalled 'antique.' So the poet mounts the pulpit, and preaches to us in a strain too rare, too little heard, too soon ended. * * * Our great poet[1] is against the age, and on the side of the morality, the religion, the virtues, which are not quoted on its stock exchange. He saw us trembling and shivering at the shadow of death like Africans, shuddering at our dead and thrusting them out of sight like Fans or Foolahs; and he wrote us the '*In Memoriam*,' a noble monument to the memory of a memory. He saw us effete, etiolated by peace, and he sounded the strains of '*Maud*' across the land, to tell us that there are worse things than war. He saw the sweet human certainties of home and household love threatened by theorists and doctrinaires, and he painted for us the noble and generous '*Princess Ida*,' ending all her dream of one-sided life with a confession, a passion, and a kiss. He observed how poor was our standard of 'a gentleman,' how easily we scrawled 'Esquire' upon our envelopes to men whose 'shield' was foul; and he created for us '*King Arthur*,' 'the spotless knight and stainless gentleman' whose solemn forgiveness, 'as God forgives,' shines like the first gleam of a great light across the highest and hardest maxim of Christianity. And now, amid our divorce courts, our Yelverton cases, our saloon scandals, and our marriage markets, he tells the story of

---

[1] Tennyson.

'*Enoch Arden.*' We leave his readers and ours to set that story, so told, against the selfishnesses of the day. * * * Fiction or fact, poetry or prose, it is a noble page of Christianity, a lesson as high above the lessons taught and practised among society as God's Heaven is above the Credit Mobilier, and his 'promises to pay' better than coupons and scrip. 'To every age,' says the Koran, ' Allah has given a teacher;' we want ours too sorely * * *."

* * * * *

I believe that, in the following pages, I have ventured on a path in literature which has not been trodden by any previous author. Many professional and popular works have been written on 'hospitals,' but none of them, as I am aware, contain a personal narrative of a patient's residence in one of them, and disclose the details of the inner-life of a large hospital from day to day.

In conclusion I may add, that if my little work prove the humble means of diffusing a knowledge of the great usefulness and importance of our general hospitals, and the claims which they have upon all classes of the community capable of affording them pecuniary assistance in the shape of donations and subscriptions, I shall feel amply recompensed for the trouble and labour which it has cost me.

A. J. C.

LONDON;
December 1*st*, 1864.

TABLE OF CONTENTS.

CHAPTER I.

PAGE

Introductory remarks on Hospitals—their great usefulness and importance—points in which they differ from other benevolent institutions—origin of the author's book . . 1—8

CHAPTER II.

The author tells his own tale—life-incidents—a January-day—how the author becomes a patient in a London hospital . 9—15

CHAPTER III.

Interior of a large hospital—arrangement and sub-divisions—wards, nurses, beds, medicines, &c.—forms of admission and treatment of patients—treatment received by the author—his first night there . . . . 16—26

CHAPTER IV.

A retrospect—stray thoughts—the past night—the morrow—incipient consciousness—sensations, day-dreams—scenes at home—watching for the absent one—the momentous letter—an angel's visit—reminiscences—evening—second night. 27—37

CHAPTER V.

PAGE

Second day and its changes—present state—senses lost and remaining—gathering clouds—abortive intentions—night and day indistinguishable—incidents—personal treatment —attending surgeons—another night and morning . . 38—45

CHAPTER VI.

Hospital-wards unattractive—a patient's diary—something about erysipelas—my third day and onward—bursting storm— thoughts and impressions—attending surgeons—visitors— concealment of true position—treatment continued—diet, medicines, and how administered—changed state—delirium —hour of parting, &c. . . . . 46—63

CHAPTER VII.

Delirium—strange thoughts and fancies—interruptions—singular visitors—early morning—day . . . . . 64—77

CHAPTER VIII.

Nocturnal rambles—Aspen-dell—temple of silence—Stonehenge — Haldon-hill — Ide-vale—fairies' home, lives, pastime, history—elves—pre-adamite world—cock-crow—dawn . 78—103

CHAPTER IX.

Strange end of a day's excursion—the Gnomes—accidental interview — some account of them — pleasant company— adventures — Ishmàiah explains difficulties — Shòphan speaks on language—Anak discourses on philosophy, discovery, and the vanity of human greatness—lost writings —Zàdok reads—old house near Leicester-square—discovery of ancient MSS.—results, &c. . . . . . 104—130

CHAPTER X.

The soul, mind, memory, imagination—sleep—death, futurity —dreams—somnambulism, somniloquism — delirium—my wanderings—operas—Cotters of the Rhine—balloon-excursion round the world—voyage of the yacht Daphne—discoveries—north-west passage—polar sea—second voyage—antarctic continent, sea, and archipelago—ancient MSS.—universal alphabet and language—extemporaneous houses—shifting of beds—restlessness, cold, sleep . . 131—159

CHAPTER XI.

Personal state and progress—crisis—subsequent debility—treatment, diet, medicines — attendants — improvement—first sense of light—daily routine—misadventure—bandages v. splints—tumefaction of head—operation—prospects—unfortunate incident, hæmorrhage — generous diet—further improvement—something to laugh at—hysterical attacks—recollections — the heart's misgivings — recovered sight, reading—learning to walk—employment of time—visitors —presents — flowers—that head again —cold-water pads, poultices—thoughts of home—progress—short relapse—scrubbing-brush Philippics—amusing incidents—approaching departure, &c. . . . . . . 160—183

CHAPTER XII.

Inner-life of a hospital—day and night in the wards—morning — prayers — breakfast—physic — round of house-surgeon and staff — passing time away—rations, bread—noon—waiting for the pot-boy—porter, stout—dinner—visiting surgeons and physicians — leisure-hours—butter—milk—tea—evening — retiring to bed— night-scenes—dietary—medicines — dispensing, &c. — Sunday — operation-day—admission-day—discharge-day—preliminaries of departure, &c. . . . . 184—205

CHAPTER XIII.

Subject continued—ward-scenes—fellow-patients—interesting cases, accident-, surgical, and medical—operations—deaths, &c. . . . . 206—226

CHAPTER XIV.

My departure from the hospital—journey home—reception and scenes there—incidents—relapse—convalescence—conclusion . . . . 227—231

APPENDIX.

ADDITIONAL NOTE	(memory)	. . . . .	232
,,	,, (dreams)	. . . . .	233—236
,,	,, (duality of mind)	. . . .	236—237
,,	,, (nurses)	. . . .	237—238
,,	,, (dietary, &c.)	. . . . .	238
,,	,, (patients)	. . . .	238—239
,,	,, (accidents)	. . . .	239

ERRATUM.

Page 6, line 2, for "Aye?" *read* "hey?"

TWO MONTHS

IN A

LONDON HOSPITAL.

CHAPTER I.

Introductory remarks on Hospitals—their great usefulness and importance—points in which they differ from other benevolent institutions—origin of the author's book.

THE mention of a "hospital," or the sight of one, commonly calls up very different thoughts in different minds. With the busy wayfarer through life, sound in health and limb, the ideas that arise, if any, have probably some confused relation to the poor and needy sick, or to the crushed or mutilated victims of street-accidents, fallen houses, or railway collisions; and so he dismisses them as uninteresting to himself. With the timid and the nervous, the mental associations perhaps embrace lazar-houses, broken limbs, hideous disfigurements, frightful surgical operations, and still more frightful experiments and tortures which idle rumour has wickedly whispered are sometimes inflicted in hospitals for the mere gratification of curiosity, or for the promotion of medical science. With the thoughtful and

benevolent, the mind probably rests on constantly recurring
instances of benefits conferred, sufferings alleviated, health
restored. In *some* of those too who have been the recipients
of these benefits—for all are not equally grateful—pleasing
remembrances not unmixed with thankfulness perhaps start
up in the mind, and feelings of sympathy for their suffering
brethren and sisters follow in their train. With the great
mass of society, however,—with the thoughtless listeners
and passers-by of all classes,—neither the 'word' nor the
'building' awakens a single generous or kindly feeling, or
even arrests the attention for a passing moment. Such
persons regard anything connected with the subject as
'slow' and 'dull' in the extreme; and any one who intro-
duces it, or who presses it on their attention, they 'vote' a
'perfect bore.' And yet of all the noble institutions with
which this metropolis abounds, there are few, or perhaps
none, which equal its public hospitals in real usefulness,
and in the ever ready, impartial, and kindly manner in
which their benefits are bestowed. In no institutions of a
benevolent character are the intentions and wishes of their
worthy founders and supporters carried out with greater
zeal, fidelity, and disinterestedness, than in them. No
political or sectarian bigotry, no difference of creed or
opinion, closes them to certain classes or parties, and opens
them to others; no arbitrary bye-laws, as in many other
kindred institutions, confine their benefits to persons of any
particular trade or profession, or grade, or age. The young
and the old, the poor and the affluent sufferer, are equally
welcome, receive equal care and attention, and hold equal
rank, there; no other qualifications being needed than
urgency for medical or surgical treatment, decorous
behaviour, and compliance with the necessary discipline of
the establishment. Even vice and crime are no disqualifi-

cations in cases of emergency or casualties. On the contrary, the dissolute and vicious, and even the hardened criminal, under proper restrictions, receive the same attention from the surgical staff as other patients; whilst their reformation and spiritual welfare is promoted by the religious instruction imparted to them by the chaplain and visitors. If a person be taken with a serious fit in the street, or be severely injured by being thrown from his horse, crushed beneath a passing omnibus, falling from a scaffold, or by any other accident, where is he generally taken by the bystanders or police? "To the nearest hospital." Yes! to the *nearest hospital;* and there, be it any hour of the day, or of the night, he *immediately* receives all the assistance which the highest surgical skill can render in his case; and there he remains, carefully nursed, attended, and provided for, until recovery enables him to return home, or until death relieves him from his sufferings. The doors of *all* our general hospitals are *always* open for the reception of cases of emergency and accident, and every possible provision is made for prompt surgical and domestic attention to the sufferers. Owing to the admirable arrangements in these institutions no delay or neglect, so injurious to such patients, can possibly occur; whilst the number of the attendants, and the completeness of the necessary appliances kept constantly at hand, place even the pauper in as good, or in a better position, under the circumstances, than that of the wealthy sufferer in his mansion.

In reference to the admission of patients suffering from disease, and which form the greater number of the 'in-patients' of every hospital, it is manifest that some regulations and some restrictions must always exist; but these, as far as the limitation of the number goes, for the most part depend on the funds and the number of beds at the disposal of the governors or trustees. Persons suffering from certain diseases, as contagious fevers, small-pox, &c., are necessarily excluded from our general hospitals, because, without separate wards and special arrangements which it would be difficult to carry out, these diseases would be liable to spread to the other patients and the surrounding district.

In reference to the 'out-patients' of our hospitals, or those who hold 'letters'[1] which entitle them to advice and medicine on attending at the institution on certain days of the week, it may be remarked, that the state of the funds and the accommodation afforded by the building, must necessarily restrict their number also, though not to the same extent as with the in-patients. In general the liberal way in which out-patient letters are distributed by the officers and contributors to our hospitals, in their desire to do as much good as possible, has rendered the duties of the dispensary department much too onerous to the medical staff, whilst those who hold them have generally to wait a very inconvenient time—often for hours—before seeing the surgeon and obtaining their medicine from the 'dispenser.' It will be seen, however, that these inconveniences are not justly attributable to the governing officers and the medical staff, but to the public, who, by the paucity of their donations and subscriptions, limit the means of the former of doing good.[2]

Much might be said on the claims of hospitals to public favour and support, and on those points which place them

---

[1] 'Letters of recommendation,' or '*recommends*' as they are usually termed by the vulgar. Advice and medicine are, however, often given without them, as observed elsewhere.

[2] The inconvenience and annoyances suffered by out-patients at our public hospitals and dispensaries were ably exposed, a short time since, in the '*Medical Circular*.'

in the very foremost rank of the benevolent and philanthropic institutions which form an essential part of the social system of our times. Illustrative examples, however, often prove more convincing and agreeable to ordinary readers than any number of mere dry statements without them; and, in many instances, may replace these last in a popular volume with manifest advantage. On the merits and demerits of the common system of employing hospitals as schools of surgery and medicine much also may be said; but being unconnected with the general object of this book, need only be alluded to here. The references to these schools that the reader may hereafter meet with, will only extend to points necessary to be known to enable him to understand details that would otherwise appear obscure.

I have been led into these remarks by certain personal incidents that occurred in a life which, if not remarkable, has been more than ordinarily eventful; and which never recur to my mind without inducing serious reflections. Soon after their occurrence I formed the determination to give them to the public in a more lengthy and formal manner than will be now attempted here; but the wise disposer of all things willed otherwise. Other circumstances arose to which I will merely allude, and prevented my carrying out the intention I had formed. I began the task I had set myself, but ere long I was compelled to leave it; and what appeared, at first, a mere temporary suspension, at length became a total abandonment of the original undertaking. And so the matter rested until a more recent date, though not without being followed, for some time, by frequently recurring moments of regret. At length an incident, of no great moment in itself, recalled the subject and pressed it on my attention. Passing through the Strand with Mr. Dudley Phipps, a wealthy country gentleman visiting London to 'lionise,' my friend, stopping suddenly and pointing towards the corner of Agar-street and King William-street, enquired, " What building is that?" "That," I replied, " is Charing Cross hospital, an excellent institution which, to me, possesses peculiar interest; and ' well it may' you say, if you would knew how my interest in it arose. I suppose you are a liberal supporter of your county hospital, and feel much interest in its affairs! Aye?" "Well!" stammered my friend carelessly, " I can't exactly say that. I generally give an annual subscription of two guineas to our hospital, and, when pressed for it, another guinea to our dispensary; but further than that I really do not trouble myself about them. *I* shall never become a patient of either."

"Two guineas a year, and no interest felt in it;" I mentally exclaimed, as we turned from the building and again entered the Strand. "Two guineas a year"—that is the money value of a wealthy man's benevolence; and even that is precisely "two guineas" more than tens of thousands of persons of ample means bestow on such institutions. " I do not trouble myself about them! *I* shall never become a patient of either!" Vain man! be not too assured of thy safety. " Boast not thyself of the morrow, for thou knowest not what a day may bring forth." A false step, a fall, a restive horse, a drunken or reckless driver, a mistaken signal, or something viewed beforehand as excessively trivial, may be the means of soon and unexpectedly laying *you*, even *you*, an agonised sufferer, on a bed in your splendid mansion, or even in the nearest hospital that you now regard as merely the refuge of the poor and friendless. However, the idea of almost absolute immunity from accidents, and more particularly from their consequences which fall so grievously heavy on the working classes and the poor, is not peculiar to Mr. Dudley Phipps, but, from pride or thoughtlessness, more or less prevails among the middle classes generally; and more among them than, perhaps, in those above them. The fallacy of such an impression will be shown and illustrated in the sequel.

We had now reached Trafalgar Square, our intention being to spend an hour or two in examining the pictures of the National Gallery. My friend's attention, however, being arrested by the fountains, we occupied about half an hour in walking up and down the terrace over them before entering the building. Whilst so engaged, and at the risk of being thought dull and tedious, I kept 'hospitals' the subject of our conversation, and endeavoured to enlist my friend's interest in them by numerous illustrative anecdotes and statements tending to shew their great usefulness and the importance attached to them by the wise and philanthropic of all civilised and christian nations. My efforts were not without results. After leaving the picture gallery the subject was mutually renewed; and on parting for the day, after dining together, I had so far interested my friend in the leading subject of our conversations, that he frankly stated he thought it possessed "much interest," and that he should "like to renew it on the first favourable opportunity." The next morning I received a note from my friend announcing the arrival in town of Mrs. Dudley Phipps (who he stated held similar opinions to my own), and warmly pressing me to join them and a small select party of friends, at his chambers in Harley-street, on each of the succeeding evenings of the week; when he hoped I should re-open the subject of 'hospitals,' and give him further details in illustration of it. I acceded to my friend's wishes, and during these visits amused our little party with a personal narrative of nearly nine weeks' residence, as a patient, in a London hospital, including the particulars of its "inner life;" a task I was the better able to accomplish from my previous long acquaintance with such institutions, though in a different and less painful position. The following chapters contain the substance of what passed on the subject during these "*Evenings in Harley-street,*" with only some slight modifications and omissions to adapt them for perusal rather than for verbal relation, and with the addition of some new matter which would have been inappropriate on the occasions alluded to. As such, gentle reader, with many apologies for their crudeness and imperfections, I present them to you in the pages of this little volume.

CHAPTER II.

The author tells his own tale—life-incidents—a January-day—how the author became a patient in a London hospital.

AFTER a long period of hard literary labour, with its accompanying seclusion and anxiety, and its common consequences—shattered nerves and injured health—I was compelled to 'doff' my dressing-gown and slippers, and to 'don' my boots and out-door apparel, in order to make certain business-visits in Town, which it was not possible for me longer to defer. It was a November-day in appearance, though in the early part of January, in which, having taken a hasty breakfast, I started from my house in Chiswick Mall by the first omnibus that passed the door. The chilliness and gloom of the morning increased as the day wore on; and, a few hours later, a cold, drizzling rain set in, which added to the cheerlessness of the scene. Dusk soon usurped the place of daylight, and evening had apparently arrived before even its usual early hour at this season of the year. The street-lamps now glared redly through the mist, and the brilliant gas-lights of the shops, as their rays struggled and darted irregularly through the streaming window-panes, deceived the eyes, instead of assisting them to penetrate the gloom. In the private streets and squares blazing fires were visible in kitchen, parlour, and drawing-room, and, as they lighted up the faces of those gathered round them, looked provokingly comfortable to the passers-by. The foot-passengers were few in number; and these hurried along, bearing umbrellas or wrapped in protective outer garments, with a discontented air, as if thoughts of home or shelter were the subjects which alone occupied their minds. And still the rain descended in a steady drizzle more searching and annoying than a downright heavy shower; whilst above an impenetrable mantle of gloom met the eye, and all around was mud and water.

Another appointment I had to keep, and two or three more calls I had to make, led me, in this inclement weather, to Woburn-square and Russel-square, and afterwards to Hart-street. This took me twice by the British Museum. On each occasion, as my eyes involuntarily rested on this building and endeavoured to trace the details of its beautiful façade through the mist, thought seemed to whisper that it would be long, very long, ere I should visit the treasures it contains again—if ever! Strange that vagrant ideas, probably occasioned by the fatigue and exposure of the day, should have been afterwards realised.

My last call was made and my business in Town finished somewhat earlier than I expected, owing to *two* of the parties in the neighbourhood just referred to being out— had even *one* of them been at home I should not be now writing this paper. I then hastened toward the Strand to 'catch' the omnibus by which I intended to ride home. In my progress thither I had to cross one of our principal thoroughfares, which was then, more than now, crowded with vehicles at this hour of the day. Along the centre of this street temporary wooden houses or sheds were erected over shafts or openings connected with the new 'Metropolitan drainage-works,' and effectually concealed the portions

of the street beyond them. These, with their huge gas-flames flaring and wavering in the mist, rendered the 'crossings' more than usually deceptive and dangerous. It was not far from one of these wooden sheds that I attempted to cross the street. The way appeared clear at the moment I left the footpath. I had partly crossed the road when I perceived the dim outline of two loaded omnibuses emerging, like grim spectres from the gloom, and approaching me at a furious space. The iron bar and chain at the head of the pole of one of them struck me, and threw me some distance in advance of it; and the next moment the iron-heels of the horses were trampling on my head, throat, and body. Then the words of Job—"My days are past, my purposes are broken off, even the thoughts of my heart"—flashed upon my mind, and seemed to assume a "local habitation" there.[1] To add to my misfortune the wheels of another loaded omnibus passing at the time ran over my projecting leg and ankle. The misconduct of the driver, who was irritated at being compelled to stop whilst his rival passed on, also contributed to aggravate the accident which his recklessness had caused. This man—with the brutal inhumanity so frequently met with in his class—kept lashing, tugging, and swearing at his horses, instead of calmly endeavouring to restrain them and keep them quiet. The by-standers who soon gathered round, looked on, but offered no assistance. The 'conductor' of the omnibus too, with equal inhumanity, merely hung round by his arm from his place behind, and gazed

---

[1] A few Sabbath-days before the time alluded to, I heard a masterly sermon delivered on this Text by the Rev. — Pearsall, which much interested me, and caused the words of Job to frequently recur to my mind. Mr. Pearsall's discourse was one of those that deserve to be printed in 'letters of gold.'

'ahead' at what was passing there, without alighting. And so three or four minutes passed, during which my feeble efforts to extricate myself proved abortive—the feet of the horses either held or struck me down on each attempt I made to raise myself. At length two gentlemen more humane and bolder than the rest appeared upon the scene, and relieved me from my perilous position. The miserable plight I was in may be better imagined than described. I have since been told that, when first extricated, I appeared little better than a mangled heap of blood, and mud, and rags. Even my boots were torn by the iron-heels of the horses; and even the stockings under them had shared the common fate.

During the whole of the time of which I have been speaking neither consciousness nor calmness materially forsook me; whilst during a part of it, the acuteness of the senses kept me cognizant of every thing that occurred around me. A minute or two later, and these senses, commencing with the eye, began to fail me. It was not, however, until some little time had elapsed that my mind lost the power of collected thought; and it was not until a still later period, to which I shall again allude, that consciousness temporarily ceased altogether. The shock and injuries I had received, followed by the continued flow of the vital stream, soon, however, did their work. A feeling of death-like lassitude and faintness, with a strong desire for rest, and a still stronger repugnance to being disturbed, came on; and the mind, as it lost the controlling influence of the senses, began to wander, as in a placid day-dream, and could only be recalled to present subjects by the strongest efforts of the will.

A military gentleman I am acquainted with has recently informed me, that a body of cavalry rushing forward to the charge, by daylight, though a startling circumstance, is not always so dangerous to the prostrate soldier lying in their track, as might be at first supposed. He had served in the Crimea, and assured me that he spoke from his personal experience whilst lying wounded on the field; and that he had heard of more than one instance that had occurred there, in which others had escaped who had been similarly exposed. He accounts for the assumed fact by the natural repugnance which, he says, exists in the horse, to treading on a human being, whom it will always clear by a leap, or by turning aside, if it possibly can. I can confirm this statement so far as a few horses in an open road or common, or the hunting-field, are concerned. But be this as it may with saddle-horses, it cannot apply to draught-horses attached to heavy vehicles and restrained by harness. In this state the natural instinct of the animal can scarcely be exercised; and to say any thing that might induce reliance on it in cases of danger, or that would lessen our watchfulness and care, would be manifestly injudicious. I can only assert from my own painful experience, that one of the most helpless, cruel, and pitiable predicaments in which a human being can be placed, is that of being knocked down and trampled on by the horses of a heavy vehicle, more particularly when either the team or vehicle is backed over his prostrate body. But to return to my narrative:—

From the spot where the accident occurred I was taken to the nearest tavern, and placed on one of the cushioned settees in its coffee-room. Here I received all the kindness and attention from the landlord, though a stranger to him, that a good Samaritan could bestow. He immediately sent for Dr. Th——, of H—— street, his family surgeon, and in two or three minutes this gentleman was at my side. His prompt attendance and kindness also deserve my special thanks. A strong stimulant was now ordered me, to support my waning strength whilst 'what should be done,' and 'where I should be taken,' was under consideration. A few minutes later, and Mr. R——,[1] also of H—— street, (a surgeon whom I had intimately known for years, and to whom I had requested one of my cards to be taken,) also arrived, and at once took charge of my case. The result of a hasty examination made by this gentleman led him to advise my immediate removal to the nearest hospital—the nature of the injuries I had received rendering it unadvisable to take me home, the distance being several miles. This he told me as he leaned over me, at the same time expressing his opinions of some of the injuries from which I was suffering. I was then placed in a cab, and, accompanied by Mr. R——, was driven from the tavern. As we left it the clock in a neighbouring steeple struck six. It fell upon my ears with a strange, booming, unearthly sound, which it never had before.

It was not long ere we reached the doors of Charing Cross hospital, although both the distance, and the time occupied by the ride, appeared very long to me. The jolting of the cab had also inflicted on me considerable torture, which, however, would have been greater, had not loss of blood and the powerful stimulant that had been administered to me considerably diminished my susceptibility to pain. I was now rapidly sinking; and by the time I was taken into the hall of the building I felt completely exhausted and almost lifeless. Here it was found necessary to again administer stimulants (brandy and sal-volatile, I believe) to sustain me whilst the apparatus was arranged for conveying me upstairs. I was then carried

---

[1] Now Dr. R——.

to a bed in the "accident-ward" of the hospital; and first the nurses, and next the surgeons, commenced their respective duties. I was now, for the first time in my life, a patient in a London hospital. And here I must leave the reader for the present. We shall meet again in a subsequent chapter.

CHAPTER III.

Interior of a large hospital—arrangement and sub-divisions—wards, nurses, beds, medicines, &c.—forms of admission and treatment of patients—treatment received by the author—his first night there.

The internal economy of all large 'general hospitals' is essentially the same—the differences, where any, being chiefly dependent on the nature or extent of the building, or confined to minor details and arrangements. In all of them the wards[1] for the reception of male and female patients are quite distinct, and usually on different floors, or in different parts of the building. A separate ward, in each set, is also usually set apart for the reception of juveniles and youth of the sex to which the department belongs. There is also usually one ward, or more, on a smaller scale, distinct from the rest, appropriated to very young children and infants of both sexes, and which, where the space is limited, are often on the upper story above the others. One, or more, of the male wards, and one at least of the female wards—the patients in the former being much the more numerous—are reserved for the reception of cases caused by accidents, and thus commonly receive the name of "accident-wards." The objects more particularly kept

---

[1] Large, lofty rooms, or separate divisions of a hospital, appropriated to in-patients.

in view in the selection of these last are—airiness, commodiousness, and ease of access. In some large hospitals there is also a further arrangement or sub-division of the wards, separate wards being devoted to surgical and medical cases, or to distinct classes of diseases. All the different wards to which I have referred, are usually, for obvious reasons, situate above the ground-floor; and, where the ground-plot is limited in extent, this is almost necessarily the case. The ground-floor itself, and the basement (if any), is required for the resident medical officers, the dispensary, surgery, board, lecture, and dissecting rooms, museum, laboratory, clerk's and other offices, dead-house, kitchens, laundry, stores, &c.

To each set of wards a 'matron' or head-nurse—in hospital parlance called "*sister*"—is appointed, with a staff of nurses under her varying in number with that of the 'beds' (patients) they have to attend to. One of these (or more occasionally), appointed specially for the purpose, is called the 'night-nurse.' Her duties usually commence about ten, and end about six or seven. The hours of the others usually extend from about seven in the morning to nine or ten at night.

The 'beds' in the wards are soft stuffed mattresses, placed on bedsteads which are usually of iron, and numbered; and at the head of each one occupied by a patient, is fixed a printed ticket bearing, in conspicuous letters, the name of one of the chief medical officers of the institution; and from this the patients become classed and known as Mr. or Dr. this or that's patients. This name, depending on the case being surgical or medical, is that of the visiting physician, or visiting surgeon, whose duty it is to go through the ward on the day the patient was admitted— each medical officer having certain fixed days of the week on which, with the house-surgeon and the pupils of his class, and accompanied by the 'sister' or matron, he goes the round of the hospital, or, in certain hospitals, of his particular wards only. Underneath the physician's or surgeon's name is written the name and address of the patient, and the date of his admission, followed by the name of the disease or injuries from which he is suffering. The last is commonly not added until some days after the patient's admission, or until the first leisure opportunity; whilst in some hospitals where the discipline is lax, it is neglected altogether. Another and larger kind of pasteboard ticket, conveniently ruled and tabulated, is hung at the head or upper corner of every bed. This contains the name of the patient, followed by the diet, and the kind and quantity of liquor (beer, wine, spirit, &c.), if any, proper in his case; as also by the prescriptions for his medicines, &c. The contents of these tickets are, of course, frequently, and sometimes even daily, altered; such alterations and additions, in surgical cases, being usually made by the house-surgeon either at the time of the periodical round of one of the visiting surgeons, or subsequently, as his judgment may dictate or the case may require. In purely medical cases these entries are usually made by the clinical clerk of the visiting physician of the day. In cases in which it is either advisable or permissible for a patient to take a little fresh-air and out-door exercise daily, such permission is also entered in his ticket.[1] He has then only to show t to the hall-porter, during the proper hours, and to leave

[1] Patients who are able to walk about freely, and even cripples, frequently ask for this privilege; and when they are orderly persons it is seldom refused them. The change of scene, and the invigorating nature of fresh air and out-door exercise, are generally found to hasten their recovery, particularly in cases of indolent sores, wounds, recently united fractures, &c.

it with him until his return, to be allowed to pass the doors.

The bed-tickets we have just noticed are extremely useful in the internal management of a hospital. Those first referred to, besides other uses, enable the medical officers to immediately recognise the beds of their respective patients, even when new ones; and they enable the nurses to answer enquiries, and to carry out the instructions given them with greater readiness and certainty. From the other tickets the 'sister' draws up her daily list of the articles and quantities of food, liquors, and other supplies, required for the patients under her charge, and which she has to sign and deliver to the storekeeper, &c., before she can obtain them. By means of them also the 'medicines' and minor 'surgical appliances' are obtained from the dispensary and store-room. For this purpose one of the nurses of the ward or set of wards, selected by the matron, collects the new and altered tickets daily (or oftener, when required), and takes them to the apothecary or dispenser, together with the empty bottles, pill-boxes, &c., of the other patients, that require re-filling.[1] After the dispenser has done his part, the nurse brings the whole of the medicines she receives back to her wards, and distributes them to the respective patients according to the names written on the labels. This she does, in the case of helpless patients, by placing the medicine on the little table, commode, or whatnot, found at the side of the head of every bed; and, in other cases, either by handing or sending the

[1] The common practice of hospital-dispensers is to write the whole prescription (in a brief form) on the labels of bottles, lids of boxes, &c.; as well as the name of the patient, the dose, &c. This saves the trouble of referring to the patient's bed-ticket every time a fresh supply is needed.

medicine to the patient, or (and more commonly) by calling out the names of the patients from the centre table on which she has emptied and disposed the contents of her basket.

In most hospitals the admission of patients suffering from ordinary diseases—surgical or medical—is limited, for the sake of convenience, to certain days of the week, and to certain hours of each day. The *days* are usually the same as those on which patients are discharged, as beds are then left unoccupied—the *hours*, subsequent to those at which the discharged patients leave the hospital, by which temporary crowding and confusion in the wards are avoided; but the last are seldom very rigidly observed, as far as I have seen. The 'forms of admission' in these cases are usually very simple. The object of the party's visit being explained to the porter on duty, he or she is at once admitted into the building. The 'recommendation' or 'order for admission'[1] being then exhibited, in turn, in the clerk's office or to the proper officer, and the patient having been seen by one of the house-surgeons, he is at once 'passed' to the appropriate ward.[2] He is then duly entered by the clerk in the 'roll' of in-patients. Soon after reaching the ward a bed is assigned the patient by the 'sister,' or one of the nurses

---

[1] In one or two of the London hospitals, I believe, recommendatory orders are not required to obtain admission as a patient, all parties approved as proper objects by the medical officers being admitted to the utmost limit the funds of the institution, and the number of vacant beds, will allow. However, a list of the donors, subscribers, and medical officers, having 'recommendations' at their disposal, may be obtained, on application, at any of the hospitals.

[2] Persons residing at a distance would do well to assure themselves before-hand that there will be a vacant bed for them on their arrival; though I never heard of any one, under such circumstances, being disappointed or refused admission.

acting for her; and in due course a card or ticket, of the kind already noticed, is attached to the head of the patient's bed. He or she is now entitled to all the benefits attached to the institution until cured, relieved, or discharged as incurable, or removed by death.

With persons suffering from 'accidents,' and in all cases of 'emergency,' the procedure connected with admission is rather different. For their reception, as already hinted, no recommendation or order is required, the doors being never closed against them, day or night. Simple cases of no great severity, such as slight wounds or burns, or bruises or contusions, broken arm or finger, dislocated elbow or wrist, and the like, are generally attended to in the surgery; and after the parts have been properly 'dressed,' or 'set' and supported by splints and bandages, or 'reduced' to their natural positions, the parties are dismissed to their homes, medicine, if required, being first given them, with orders to attend again at the hospital on certain days of the week. In recent cases of simple dislocation of the shoulder, the parties, for greater convenience, are usually taken to the 'accident-ward,' and the operation of reduction is performed on one of the beds there; after which, either at once, or in a few hours, they also are dismissed. In more serious cases, as severe accidents and injuries, sudden fits of apoplexy, strangulated hernia, suspended animation or wounds from attempted suicide, &c., the mode of procedure assumes a corresponding character. On a patient being brought in a helpless state (say in a cab or other vehicle) to the hospital, he is carried into the hall or lobby of the building, and at once placed in a kind of large chair kept ready for the purpose. The rope of the 'accident-bell'—a large bell mounted in an appropriate part of the inner side or back of the building—is now vigorously pulled, to announce to the medical staff the arrival of an 'accident-case,' and to put the nurses of the accident-ward on the 'qui vive' so as to prepare for his arrival there. The chair just referred to is so formed that it may be readily adapted to either the sitting or recumbent posture, with a movable attachment in front to support, when required, a broken limb in a horizontal position. It is carried by means of long removable handles or poles, in a similar way to a Bath-chair. The house-surgeon and his assistants are usually by this time at the side of the patient, and render such assistance as they can whilst these preliminary proceedings are going on. As soon as the poles or handles are fixed in their places, and the patient disposed in as comfortable a position as the circumstances will permit, the bearers[1] start with their burthen, and in a minute or two have reached the male or female accident-ward, as the case may be. The patient is then assisted or lifted to one of the beds pointed out by the 'sister' or one of the nurses, in whose charge he is left. Persons brought on 'stretchers,' as they are called, or the like, are at once carried on them to the accident-ward, without removal.

As soon as a patient has reached his bed in the accident-ward of a hospital, the duties of the nurses commence. His clothes are now gently removed, but with as much expedition as possible. The wounds or injured parts are next freed from blood and mud by means of a sponge and

---

[1] These are usually the porter on duty, with one or other of the male servants of the hospital or one of the able-bodied patients of the male wards. With parties brought in by working-men—particularly by their fellow-workmen—this duty is generally performed by them. I have often been pleased to see the readiness with which such men will leave their work to assist a suffering brother, and the kindness they have shewn him. Policemen bringing in cases also often readily and kindly do this duty.

warm water; and the whole body, if dirty, cleansed with warm soap-and-water in a similar manner. One of the house-surgeons, and one or more of his staff, are already present. A rigid surgical examination of the case is made, the nature of the injuries determined, and their surgical treatment began. It is now that dislocations are 'reduced,' broken bones 'set' and supported with splints and bandages, wounds sewed up or 'dressed,' protruding parts replaced, &c. In these cases, if any operations of a delicate character have to be performed, a large winged screen is placed round the patient's bed, by which privacy is obtained and interruption prevented. If any severe operation that demands immediate attention is required—as, for instance, that for dislocation of the thigh, or for the removal of a limb—the patient is generally removed to the 'operation-room' or 'theatre,' for the purpose; but if there be no urgency in the case, the matter is deferred to a more convenient period —probably the next day, or even the general 'operating-day' of the week. The immediate surgical treatment of the case being over, the patient's body-linen is replaced, or, if necessary, fresh linen or a 'neck-blanket' is supplied him by the 'sister.' The proper medicines, if any are required, are next, in due course, administered, and the patient is left to repose. Henceforth his case, subject to the demands peculiar to it, falls under the usual routine, surgical and domestic, of the hospital. In the mean time, or soon afterwards, the clothes removed from the patient are collected together by one of the nurses, and, with any other things belonging to him, are placed, for safe-keeping and convenience, in the large drawer which is usually attached to the foot of each bedstead. If he be thoroughly helpless, or insensible, money, jewelry, or other valuables found on him at the time of undressing him, are usually taken charge of by one of the house-surgeons, or the 'sister,' two lists of them being at the same time made, in the presence of a witness, one of which is retained by the surgeon, and the other handed to the clerk of the hospital, or to the police, if one of them be present.

My own case belonged to the category of those noticed in the last two paragraphs. "How I got there," I have already told the reader; and "what subsequently passed there" on that eventful evening, he will probably, by this time, be able to anticipate. To relate all the details would involve needless repetitions. I will, therefore, confine myself to a few personal particulars:—

Before I had reached the accident-ward a sort of dreamy stupor came over me, and a vague sense of being borne forward and upward is all that I can recollect of my passage there. From this I was partially aroused by a draught of cold air blowing on me from one of the ventilators and an adjacent open window of the ward, and by being undressed. The only care I exhibited during this process, and the only subject on which I recollect speaking, was in respect to the safety of a parcel of MS. I had with me, and which I had never parted hold of except, for a single moment, when one of the horses set his foot on the hand that grasped it. My earnest desire now was for repose. I felt I must have this, and for this I could have sacrificed every thing. My only desire was to be left alone, although my tongue failed to express the words. The blood and mire were quickly removed from my person in the manner previously described, and my wounds exposed to view; a duty which was skilfully and gently performed by Mrs. D——, the 'sister' of the ward, assisted by one of the nurses. The surgical examination was now made by Mr. D——tte, one of the house-surgeons: and immediately afterwards this gentleman and one of his assistants commenced the surgical treatment of my case. This was necessarily lengthy and tedious; and, in some part of it, extremely painful and trying, not to use a stronger word. Had it not been for the lessened sensibility from loss of blood, and the injuries and shock I had received, it would have been worse. However, I did not flinch or murmur. I knew it was unavoidable, and was perfectly resigned and patient. And here my feelings compel me to record the great kindness and tenderness shewn by Mr. D—— towards me, and the skilled delicacy with which he performed his trying duties. I perceived and appreciated it all at the time; and the admiration of those who witnessed it was frequently expressed to me at a subsequent period of my sojourn in the hospital. The words of sympathy, encouragement, and hope, which he then whispered in my ear whilst stooping over me, are still fresh in mind, and will never be forgotten by me. I still well remember the soothing tones of his voice as he thrust the cruel needle loaded with silver-wire through my flesh whilst sewing my ear to my cheek, and whilst drawing together the fearful wound in my throat. Even the pain of an operation may be lessened by the kindness, sympathy, and manipular skill of him who performs it; and these—all these—I was so fortunate as to meet with on this unfortunate occasion. During this trying period the continued loss of blood, together with the severe shock received by the nervous system, rendered it necessary to several times administer stimulants to prevent my sinking under them. At length, my wounds being sewed up and 'dressed,' and my fractures 'set' and bandaged, I lay on my back in a large London hospital, a helpless victim of a street-accident of more than ordinary severity. My features by this time, as I was afterwards told, appeared thoroughly bloodless, and had assumed so cadaverous a hue, that some of those around me were uncertain whether I was living or dead. What further happened on that eventful evening, as far as my knowledge extends and memory can recall, may be told in very few words. Exhaustion did its work, and consciousness of external things each moment lessened. I endeavoured to open my eyes. It appeared a task of herculean labour, so heavy had their lids become. At length they opened, and then I perceived that I was blind. The discovery, however, did not alarm me, or even move my feelings. I felt conscious it was so, that it was to be so, and that it was the will of God it should be so. The words of Job, "My days are passed, my purposes are broken off, even the thoughts of my heart," again rushed into my mind, and, as it were, on some huge written tablet, kept floating before it with gradually waning distinctness. A degree of mental serenity and physical quiet ensued, which could only be understood by those who have experienced it; and to which the words of Martial, referring to sleep,

"How sweet alive in living death to lie;
"And without dying, ah! how sweet to die!"—

might not inaptly be applied. And so I lay, perfectly calm and motionless—how long I cannot tell—until objective sense had completely passed away, and I had fallen into a state which was neither consciousness nor insensibility, sleep nor death, but closely akin to each of them—a state in which the soul, as it were, no longer recognising its connection with the body, seemed floating in subdued and holy light that formed the boundary of another world. At length, even this state passed into one of obscurity and utter senselessness, and memory can record no more.

CHAPTER IV.

A retrospect—stray thoughts—the past night—the morrow—incipient consciousness—sensations, day-dreams—scenes at home—watching for the absent one—the momentous letter—an angel's visit—reminiscences—evening—second night.

A RESIDENCE in London during the greater portion of my life, and a daily acquaintance for many years with its chief centres of business and traffic, had so familiarised me with the bustle and confusion of its crowded streets, that a thought of danger to myself in passing through them scarcely ever entered my mind. And yet I had seen many street accidents; and I had often cautioned others, particularly members of my own family and visitors to this great metropolis, to be careful and vigilant on this point. Had the like advice been given to myself, at that time, I should probably have received it with a smile, and should thus have fallen into the category of those whom I have censured in a previous chapter. But so it is. Indeed one of the commonest failings of human nature is to give that advice to others which we ourselves neglect, or think we do not need. In our thoughtless self-reliance we commonly forget the venerable proverb that "the pitcher that goeth often to the well is likely to come home broken at last." And so it was with me. With a fervent belief in an overruling and almighty providence that "shapes our ends, rough-hew them as we will," and with a lively knowledge and conviction of the awful truth that "in the midst of life we are in death," the eagerness and absorption of my mind in the matters more immediately before it on the eventful day with which our narrative begins, excluded almost every other thought. Had it been otherwise, the idea of personal danger in a ride of only a few miles, and in a few hours devoted to business in London, would undoubtedly have been one of those the least likely to occur to me. I had left my home in the morning, if not in health, at least with the feelings of confidence, of hope and trust, that commonly animate the mind of one who is strongly bent on the fulfilment of objects of business and duty. The changeful kaleidoscope of life soon, however, developed the painful scene of the evening, already noticed. And the night passed away, and the morrow came—the morrow of that hopeful yestermorn—the morrow of that dreadful yestereve —and where was I?—what was I now?—

"Prostrate laid—
"A helpless entity; human in form;
"Scarce conscious, and bereft of half the senses:—
"Fit spectacle to curb the pride of fools,
"And bid them pause and think."

The interval between the point at which the last chapter closes and the following day, was a blank in my existence. The hours of that long winter-night came and passed away, and found and left me in a state of complete unconsciousness. The utmost efforts of recollection fail to revive a single idea or incident connected with that period. It was not until the morning had far advanced, and the noise and bustle of the day were at their height, that partial consciousness began to return. Its dawn resembled the mental condition often occurring to persons ere they fully awake from sleep, after sound sleep has passed away; in which obscure, wandering ideas float through the mind, and of which a sense of the house or the street being astir forms a part. I now became sensible of strong gusts of wind blowing on my head and face, and rambling thoughts connected with winds and tempests followed. The sound of water rushing from the taps in the adjoining wash-house, of which the door opened nearly opposite my bed, carried my mind away to the falls of Terni, the cataracts of Niagara, and other like scenes which I had visited. These thoughts and scenes though obscure, transient, and disconnected, seemed to jostle on each other in the most perplexing confusion. Then the ceaseless hum of voices and the noise of rushing vehicles reached me from the busy street—a Babel of sounds which, uninterpretable by me, suggested a thousand thoughts, among which gorgeous pageants, the roar of crowds, the roll of artillery, and the sough of distant waves, had places. Gradually I became conscious of persons moving about and of voices near me; and I had a vague sense of being touched and spoken to. I was, however, unable to answer then; or, indeed, even to make an effort to do so. Soon other thoughts came crowding on me—thoughts of home and those I loved there. I listened. I tried to call to those I was accustomed to have around me; but no one answered me. By degrees my mind conceived the fact—I was not at home! Where was I then? I tried to think; but my efforts to answer the question which my mind suggested, for a long time proved abortive. Whilst endeavouring to collect my thoughts on the subject, they wandered away to something else. I tried to rouse myself; but for some time my efforts were vain. I opened my eyes—a work of labour. Around me seemed a gloomy void, in which the only thing perceptible was an object at a little distance above me which resembled a piece of iron or coal as it appears at a dull red-heat. It was one of the gas-lights of the ward, kept burning on that gloomy winter-day. The discovery partially recalled my shattered senses, and a similar one that I had made on the preceding evening. Then confused ideas of where I was, and how I came there, crowded into my mind, and roused me to semi-consciousness. But blessed be God, for He " tempers the wind to the shorn lamb." He who had permitted me to be struck down with affliction and brought nigh unto death, had, in His mercy, sent me a palliative to enable me to bear the blow. My usually excitable and nervous temperament had left me; and I had become, for the time, mentally impassive, though not indifferent to the calamities that had befallen me. Had it been otherwise, the physical sufferings that accompanied returning consciousness, augmented by mental anguish, would have overwhelmed me. As yet my injuries and their consequences had scarcely arrested my attention. The state which I was in had rendered them nearly imperceptible. Soon, however, a strange feeling of languor and uneasiness, and a sense of utter helplessness came over me, and gradually increased in intensity, until they approached to torture. My brain appeared to be 'swimming,' my head unusually large and heavy, and as if a dense fog or mist surrounded it. Then pain—local pains—supervened, and every injury I had received became momentarily more afflictive. An iron-band seemed compressing my throat and chest, ready to crush me; and every act of respiration gave me pain. It was the bandages that thus affected me. I attempted to turn my head. The effort failed; and the extreme pain it caused me in my throat and neck, recalled my thoughts to the wounds there. I tried to raise my arm. It was powerless, and tightly bandaged to my side and chest. I could not perceive that I had any right hand, or where the fore-arm terminated. They had lost sensation owing to the pressure and contracted position to which they were subjected. After searching for some time with the other hand, as well as my feeble strength permitted, I found the lost one extended across the upper part of my chest, near my neck, and tightly held there by bandages. Next my hip and thigh arrested my attention; the one by the severe intermitting pain felt there; the other, by the absence of sensation in it. Then the dull, throbbing pains in my injured leg and ankle changed, at intervals, into lance-like spasms; and a torturing sensation in the part, as of being exposed to extreme cold, induced rigors which gradually extended upward to my body. It seemed as if the limb were lying on a bed of cold iron or marble, with ice around it, and nothing to shield it from the effects of a freezing atmosphere. This arose from its being laid on a piece of polished oil-cloth, and being covered with cold-water dressings, whilst a waggon-head 'guard' or frame of ironwork was placed over it, to prevent the bedding getting wet, and to allow of the more frequent and convenient renewal of the dressings. Those only who have been exposed to the lengthened application of ice or very cold water, under similar circumstances, can correctly estimate the intolerable sensations it induces. I tried to relieve myself by endeavouring to raise the limb, and by shuffling it about; but my strength was unequal to either. Collected thought had left me; or rather, had not yet returned. My mind, at this time, in relation to the body, might, indeed, be compared to an infant in swaddling clothes, unable to direct itself, only feebly guided by objective sense, and only vaguely conscious of its own existence. And so I lay—now roused by pain, now sinking into partial unconsciousness; and, for the most part, with my thoughts rambling as in a day-dream, and often on subjects utterly unconnected with myself, or with the circumstances immediately surrounding me. And thus my first day in a London hospital passed away, relieved, as far as I can recollect, by only two or three incidents of sufficient interest to deserve a notice here.

I have already mentioned that, on the previous evening, I requested my friend, Mr. R—, to at once send and inform my wife of my accident, and where I had been taken. This, it appears, he did immediately on his arrival home. His letter, however, did not reach its destination until late the following morning. My wife, as well as the other members of my family, including my faithful dog, watched for me, in a dreadful state of anxiety all night, and until the arrival of this letter. During these hours of watching, as I have since been informed, every footstep approaching the house they imagined must be mine; and not once, but frequently, they rushed to the door to welcome, as they thought, the truant home. On these occasions, ending in disappointment, none exhibited greater activity, and greater grief, than the sagacious dog. Darting to the garden-gate, he would strain his eyes through the darkness in the direction of the approaching sound, and then, looking at his mistress, utter a mournful whine, and turning toward the house, endeavour to induce her to follow him. Often too would he start up and listen to some sound unheard by others, and then surlily resume his place by the side of his mistress, to whom he expressed his grief and disappointment by unmistakeable signs. I so seldom went out of doors at this period, and even when I visited Town so constantly returned at an early hour, that when midnight had passed, the anxiety respecting me changed into misgivings that something unforeseen and calamitous had happened to me. As the small hours of early morning came and passed away, a strong impression almost amounting to conviction haunted Mrs. C——'s mind that such was actually the case. Indeed, so strong were her feelings on the subject that, long before daylight came, she got herself ready to at once respond to any summons she might receive to attend elsewhere, or to act on any intelligence she might be able to obtain. The delivery of the letter just referred to disclosed the mystery of my absence. It was cautiously worded in order to avoid giving unnecessary alarm. The writer briefly stated that "owing to an accident having befallen Mr. C——, he had thought it advisable to have him removed to Charing-cross hospital, where he then was; but that he hoped it was not serious, and trusted that in a few days Mr. C—— would be able to again return home." Thus the fears of the night were realised by the event announced in this letter; and the acute perception of an affectionate and faithful wife soon convinced her that the kind feelings of the writer had led him to conceal the worst features of the case. Him whom it referred to might be dead or dying. She would instantly fly to his side, ascertain the truth for herself, and do what she could for him She would try to save him. Her anxiety on the subject filled her with dread—dread that she might reach him too late.

Mrs. C—— started by the first conveyance she could meet with; and sometime before noon found herself at the doors of the hospital. She had never before had occasion to visit such a building, and she was wholly ignorant of the proper method of proceeding to obtain admission to see a patient. Her feelings, however, led her on and gave her energy, and without stopping she crossed the steps and entered the hall. Here she encountered the hall-porter, whom she requested to direct her where to find Mr. C——, who had been brought there the previous evening. The man told her it was not the day on which patients were allowed to be visited by their friends, and that she must come again to-morrow, between two and four o'clock. She then requested to see one of the medical officers of the institution, and in a few minutes was introduced to Mr. T——,* the house-surgeon in chief. She stated her business to him, and repeated her request. At first he politely told her that the state I was in rendered it unadvisable, and even dangerous, for me to be disturbed by visitors; but on her acquainting him with her name and the near relationship between us, he at once, and in the kindest manner, directed her to be shown to the accident-ward where I lay, at the same time cautioning her not to excite me by giving way to her feelings, nor to otherwise disturb me. He then gave orders to the porter to admit her, without interruption, whenever she came; and henceforth, during my stay at the hospital, she had the entrée there. A minute or two later, and she was at my bedside. Then I had an obscure perception of a familiar voice close to me. It was that of my wife speaking to the nurse. Soon I felt the touch of a soft light hand upon my forehead, and perceived that some one was leaning over me. I could faintly distinguish a dim and shadowy outline, as of a bonnet close to my face. Then my wandering thoughts were recalled to time and home by a pressure of the hand, and a gentle voice saying in my ear—" My poor, dear A——, I am come to nurse you, and to pray for you. God bless and help you! I am by your side now! Do you know me, A——?" I feebly responded her christian name; on which, still leaning over me, she said " My dearest A——, trust in God! *He* will not desert you! He will support us through this dreadful trial! I am with you now. *I* too

---

[1] Now Dr. T——.

will never desert you." Nor did she, as the reader will find in the sequel, together with the melancholy consequences of this noble self-devotion. She next communicated with the "sister" of the ward, and with the nurse who had charge of me, and learned from them all the then known particulars of my case, as well as various matters connected with the routine of the hospital. With another expressive touch of the hand, and a few more kind words uttered in my ear, she left me for a time, in order to visit and see certain members of my family that it was absolutely necessary immediately to communicate with. This business over she was again by my side, and did not leave me until a late hour in the evening. Henceforth, until a few days before I left the hospital, she was with me daily, from early in the morning to the latest hour at night that it was possible for her to remain in the ward. In the interval between leaving the hospital at night and returning to it the next morning, she attended to various domestic affairs that required her superintendence, and had to travel upwards of thirteen miles, thus leaving herself little time for rest and sleep. Such were the sacrifices voluntarily made by this noble-minded and faithful woman in the path of affection and duty.

My old friend, Mr. R——, also kindly called to see me this morning, and repeated his visit almost daily for some time afterwards. I believe I also had some other visitors during the day, but I do not remember their names.

Of other circumstances that occurred this day, I have only a faint remembrance. Some of them left no permanent impression on my mind; and others, of little interest, I have become acquainted with since. Among the first I recollect being examined by the surgeon I have already noticed as having attended me on the preceding evening, accompanied, I believe, by Mr. T——, the principal house-surgeon, and by others; as also of being raised up in bed whilst a cup or glass containing liquid—whether medicine or food I do not now remember—was placed to my mouth. I also recollect my wife speaking to me two or three times after her return, and her words at parting, on leaving me for the night—how she hung over me, and with christian fervour uttered in my ear a prayer that God would have mercy on me, and save me, and heal my wounds, and restore me to strength and health; or that if, in his wisdom, he willed otherwise, that he would take me to himself, and give me an inheritance in his everlasting kingdom, where "the wicked cease from troubling, and the weary are at rest;" where faith assured her she should join me, to pass a blissful eternity together.

I may here mention that, after the morning, much of the day was passed in a state of drowsiness approaching coma, in which pain and sense were, for the most part, lost or greatly lessened; and from which I was only occasionally aroused by loud noises, or by words addressed directly to my left ear. This state arose from the injuries to my head; and from my right ear having been almost torn off, and from the blows and wounds on the side of my face and throat having rendered the internal ear on that side insensible to sound. As the evening approached the languor, pains, and restlestness of the morning, again returned, and roused me; and to these were added feverishness and a peculiar sensitiveness of the skin of my whole body, which aggravated the irksomeness of lying helpless in a prostrate position. The noises too around me, though less distinctly heard than before, began to annoy and pain me. The rattling of the doors, the continued roll of passing vehicles in the street, and the ceaseless hum of the busy crowd there, seemed to have assumed new sounds, now grating on my ear like horrid discords, and now assuming a dull, unearthly character such as I had never heard before. This early exacerbation and change of character in the symptoms, were medical prognostics of the disease that was shortly about to afflict me. As the night wore on all these symptoms and their attendant sufferings increased in severity, and probably did not reach their climax until after midnight, when the exhaustion following long restlessness and suffering began to do its work. It was not, however, until the noise of passing carriages had ceased in the adjoining street—which, as I afterwards learned, does not usually occur until two in the morning—that I fell into a fitful feverish sleep, if I may so call the intermittent half-delirious, half-comatose state, produced by the exhaustion following long restlessness and pain. An hour or two later, and this state was relieved by the access of absolute lethargy or coma, which completed my second night, and carried me far into my second day in a London hospital.

CHAPTER V.

Second day and its changes—present state—senses lost and remaining—gathering clouds—abortive intentions—night and day indistinguishable—incidents—personal treatment—attending surgeons—another night and morning.

RESUMING my narrative at the point at which the last chapter closes, I must again trouble the reader with some personal details of a minor, though painful character. On being aroused—it cannot be said, awakened—by the noise and bustle around me the next morning, my feelings and condition were not materially changed in character from those of the preceding day. This change, however, though little, was in a downward direction, and with the new symptoms that gradually developed themselves, indicated, to the skilled eye of my medical attendants, the malignant disease that was about to follow. The stitches that held the wound in my throat together were now annoyingly perceptible; whilst those that retained my ear in its place occasioned me much pain and irritation. The scalp had grown extremely tender, and I had a distinct perception of its existence which it is difficult to explain. It seemed to envelope and rest on the skull like a warm, close-fitting, soft cap. At every act of respiration the ragged ends of my fractured collar-bone appeared to grate harshly and audibly together. The pressure of my injured ribs was painfully perceptible on the lungs beneath them. My skin had increased in dryness, heat, and sensitiveness; so much so, that the inequalities of the mattress and the wrinkles in the sheet on which I lay, began to annoy me. All my injuries, and these were numerous, disturbed me more than they had on the previous day; whilst the pain in some of them came on at shorter intervals, and in severer paroxysms. Every bandage and dressing seemed to have become tighter, or more annoying and less endurable. As the day wore on, all these symptoms and sufferings increased in severity and distinctness, and others supervened. The skin, particularly of my head, neck, and chest, continued to increase in sensitiveness and became affected with new sensations which I am unable correctly to describe. The 'cuticle' or outer skin seemed to lie on the surface of the 'cutis' or true skin like a thin, soft, flexible, but unyielding pellicle; whilst the existence of the latter as an enveloping attachment to the body, above the flesh or muscles, was distinctly perceptible. This was accompanied by a peculiar kind of irritation which was neither itching nor tingling, nor a creeping sensation, but somewhat resembled a combination of them in which the last predominated. The only sensation to which I can at all compare it, is that accompanying rubefaction produced by the application of a strong solution of iodine or strong acetic acid. These sensations, which increased *in dies*, nay hourly, were not, at first, exactly painful in themselves, but caused excessive restlessness which was worse than pain. Soon, however, they became a source of pain and intolerable annoyance, from the exquisite sensibility of the skin that accompanied them. The state of my mind too was gradually changing its character from that of the preceding day. I still lay, for the most part, in an apparently drowsy or lethargic state, only varied by the restlessness caused by pain, and by that common to such cases; but thought and imagination were rapidly acquiring more activity, though their operations and sequences were irregular, discursive, and generally disconnected. The chief 'gateways' of knowledge and perception were more or less closed or obstructed, and thus the controlling influence of objective sense was, for the most part, lost to the mind. 'Sight' had departed for a season; 'hearing' had become so defective and confused, that except during occasional moments of laborious attention, it afforded only vague suggestions for the thoughts and imagination to riot on; whilst the sense of 'touch,' from its exalted and disorganised condition, tended to distress me, and to lead the mind astray. I was, however, still capable of collected thought at intervals which, though short, were frequently recurring. My feeble mind also appreciated, though somewhat vaguely, the position I was in; and was intermittingly occupied with thoughts of home and those I loved there. I had much to communicate to my wife who, though I could not see her, I was sensible was sitting by my side—certain wishes to express to her—certain directions and advice to give her—all of which I resolved, as I also did almost daily afterwards for some time, to attend to before she left me for the night. But my condition precluded my carrying my intentions out. The subject was continually recurring to my mind, but my thoughts were inconstant, and my ability insufficient for the purpose. The anxiety and grief that afflicted me as the nightly hour of parting approached, dispelled the subject altogether for a time. After a short interval it would again recur to my mind, and then I bitterly reproached myself for my forgetfulness and imbecility. On these occasions I mentally exclaimed with Job, "My days are past; my purposes are broken off; even the thoughts of my heart." Indeed I was now both physically and mentally a mere wreck of my former self—a mere embodiment of passivity helplessly dependent on others. Even the distinction between night and day was no longer directly perceptible to me. My knowledge of their respective existence and recurrence was only derived from other occurrences by an act of reflection and memory, which often failed me, and left me wandering in doubt on the subject.

My wandering attention, as I have already hinted, was frequently occupied with my own condition; not because I was oppressed by fear or anxiety on the subject, but from a life-long habit of observation having given its bias to my mind. My medical knowledge soon led me to regard my symptoms as the harbingers of impending erysipelas. I duly estimated the critical position I was in; and with the calmness induced by habitual reliance on the goodness and mercy of a God "too wise to err, too good to be unkind," looked forward unmoved on what I conceived would inevitably happen. "Thy will be done!" "Thy ways are just and right!" "A broken and a contrite heart, O God, thou wilt not despise;" were among the disjointed sentences that rose from my heart to the throne of mercy when this conclusion was formed. During the greater portion of the day after the morning, however, my mind was chiefly occupied by a succession of what I can only compare to quiet day-dreams suggested by the various sounds around me— a certain prelude to the peculiar delirium that always accompanies the severer forms of erysipelas. As the evening approached my consciousness of pain considerably declined. The intervals of repose were longer, and the attacks less severe, or less heeded. The cold-water dressings on my leg and ankle, and the peculiar condition of my skin, were the objects that now chiefly distressed me, and kept me in a state of wretched restlessness.[1] And now my wandering thoughts ventured on bolder and wilder flights; and as the night set in every sound that fell confusedly on my ear, set my imagination rioting over scenes and stories of its own creation, or over by-gone incidents which it reproduced in every possible variety of form and hue. This was incipient delirium. With the progress of the disease it soon assumed the well-marked and peculiar forms which I shall presently notice.

Of the hospital scenes occurring around me this day I have little to record. The "ruling passion" which, we are told, is "strong in death," appears also to exist in illness as far as the condition of the patient will allow. At least it was so in my case, as I have hinted above. The habit of observing and investigating everything that arrested my attention, of collecting data, drawing inferences, and recording results in my mind, had been to me one of the chief sources of pleasure from my childhood up, and it was not wholly lost to me now. I still continued intuitively to observe and reason at intervals, though in a loose and imperfect way. This was only what might be expected; for the habits of a life can never be wholly lost. Sometimes I made extraordinary efforts to keep my attention and thoughts on one particular subject; but the attempt was generally idle, from other subjects rising in my mind and destroying the continuity of thought on the original one. This state, during my more lucid intervals, arose not merely from the weak and disorganised condition of my mind, but also from the materials furnished me by my shattered senses being meagre and deceptive, and suggesting new trains of thought which, for a time, replaced the previous

[1] The like dressings on my throat and head did not annoy me; probably from the circulation being more vigorous there.

ones. It was thus that the scenes occurring around me recognisable, in my case, only by the sounds that accompanied them, were perceived by me, and affected me. The chief incidents in the ward that attracted my notice during the day were connected with the violent behaviour, shoutings, and absurd language, often ludicrous, which I afterwards found came from certain patients labouring under that most disgraceful of all diseases—'delirium tremens' or the madness of drunkards. The like also occurred almost daily for some time afterwards.

Of my personal treatment this day, and the incidents connected with it, I can remember little worth mentioning. The reminiscences of my mental state and operations at that time are now fuller and stronger than those concerning what was done to me by others; and it is natural, for obvious reasons, that this should be the case. My confidence in the skill, kindness, and attention, of those in whose hands I then was, precluded any anxiety or care on my part on the matter, even had I been otherwise disposed to indulge in such feelings. I recollect that on this day, as on those that followed it, I was early visited by the surgeon who attended me on the evening of my arrival at the hospital; and subsequently, both by him and Mr. T——the chief house surgeon, on their usual 'round' through the wards. I also recollect that on this second visit I was raised in bed, and gently and carefully examined; that my bandages and dressings were replaced by fresh ones, my injuries and the parts adjacent that required it cleansed from blood, and that before these little matters were completed faintness had so far come over me that consciousness was nearly lost. The first named of the above gentlemen also visited me several times later in the day, and seemed to feel the most lively interest in my case. Although I could not see his features I recognised him by his voice, and was otherwise conscious of his presence. I did not know even his name then; but soon obtained it, through my wife, from the nurse. I could not, however, remember it long together, as it was an unusual one and new to me; although I was anxious to do so, for I fully appreciated his great kindness and felt grateful to him for it. This forgetfulness on my part led me so frequently to enquire for his name, that I became really ashamed of my imbecility. I had also some other professional visitors, apparently attracted by the novelty of my case; but with the exception of two or three whom I had previously known, I am not acquainted with their names. I now became aware that I was a patient of Mr. H. H——, the eminent operative surgeon, and one of the chief visiting surgeons of the hospital; having been brought there on the evening of Tuesday, one of the days of the week on which he goes the round of the wards. He had not, however, seen me yet; and I felt anxious that he should do so. The subject was revived in my mind with almost every visit I received, and was followed by the enquiry—"That is Mr. H—— then?" Later in the day the impression grew upon me that he had seen me; but on telling my nurse so, was disappointed to find that I had mistaken some one else for him. She assured me that he had not been in the ward since I was brought into it.

I have now carried the reader through the day, and into he early hours of my second night in a London hospital. He may probably be already aware, that patients affected with fevers, and with most other diseases of a severe inflammatory character, are subject to periodical exacerbations of the symptoms, of which the most marked commence at the approach of night. During the day there is usually a remission of the symptoms, or at least of their severity, and even comparative ease and comfort may be enjoyed; yet with the return of night they reappear, or increase in violence, until the crisis be passed. It is then that the pulse acquires increased force and rapidity, that languor changes into feverish excitement, that the feeling of restlessness and uneasiness becomes intolerable, and that delirium is first exhibited, or if it has been previously present, assumes a more aggravated and distressing form. This state commonly begins to subside soon after midnight, but does not wholly disappear until some time later in the early morning. It is succeeded by a wretched state of languor and exhaustion, from which the patient gradually sinks into unrefreshing sleep or stupor which continues several hours. My own case was no exception to the general rule. Night brought with it the increased restlessness and uneasiness referred to. The mind bursting the control of the will and senses, rambled amidst scenes of calm or beauty of its own creation, which it clothed in peculiar light, dissimilar to any thing in the material world. At last, even the very bed on which I lay grew intolerable, and every bandage, and particularly the cold-water dressings, grew the same. These sometimes gave a tone to my mental wanderings or dreams; but more frequently, the varying intensity of the one subdued the other. Then came a period of exhaustion ending in sleep or stupor, in which the operations of both mind and sense were equally suspended; and in this state I entered on another day.

CHAPTER VI.

Hospital-wards unattractive — a patient's diary — something about erysipelas — my third day and onward — bursting storm — thoughts and impressions — attending surgeons — visitors — concealment of true position — treatment continued — diet, medicines, and how administered — changed state — delirium — hour of parting, &c.

THE ward of a hospital is not a place that persons usually delight to linger in, nor do the details of a patient's case from day to day exhibit those varying novelties which appear to be necessary to render a narrative attractive. Even those whom duty or kindness calls there, are generally glad to escape as soon as possible from its painful scenes and gloomy atmosphere, and to forget, in the busy world outside it, the objects which had temporarily engaged their attention, and, perhaps, awakened their interest and sympathy. A patient's diary, if extending over any length of time, must undoubtedly possess a tedious sameness, involving a number of details and statements which, though actually varying from day to day, present to the popular eye such trifling shades of difference, as to appear mere repetitions of what has gone before. They may thus swell its bulk, but add nothing to its usefulness and interest. And this is more particularly so with a patient both physically and mentally prostrated, whose diminished senses and energies limit his observations to the narrow circle of his own bed, and his immediate attendants. Even the medical description of a case containing, as it necessarily does, the particulars of the patient's state, with the varying details of the symptoms and treatment daily, proves dull and tedious to other than professional readers. Why this is so, it appears scarcely necessary to consider here. In pursuing my narrative I shall endeavour to avoid, as much as possible, the common causes of dulness and tediousness just indicated. This I shall try to do by confining myself to the leading circumstances and incidents—the salient angles of the case,—more particularly those which, though of a personal character, appear of general interest and application, and best illustrate hospital-life. My progress, however, will not be unaccompanied by misgivings that, with some persons, my best efforts to interest them, will, owing to the nature of the subject, prove unsuccessful.

Most of my readers have heard of 'erysipelas,'[1] the 'St. Anthony's fire'[2] of old writers and the vulgar; but probably only a few of them know the nature of the disease to which these names are given. I will tell them something about it. Erysipelas is a peculiar diffused inflammation which chiefly attacks the skin. It is generally accompanied by much tumefaction, and by an eruption of a fiery red colour, not unfrequently vesicular. There is also much fever and constitutional excitement, and usually delirium or coma. Its common seat is the head and face; but no part of the surface of the body is exempt from its attacks. In its severer forms it is usually attended with typhoid symptoms, and is then a dangerous and often a fatal disease. In these cases the tumefaction of the scalp is commonly accompanied or followed by suppuration. The disease is usually at its height from the third to the sixth day; and

[1] From the Greek, ερυσιπελας.
[2] So called from the belief that it was cured by the intercession, or by the touch, of St. Anthony.

from the eighth to the twelfth day, the 'cuticle' or scarf-skin generally comes off in scales or scabs, leaving the surface under it of its natural colour, but highly delicate and sensitive. The duration and progress of the symptoms are, however, very variable, and often persistent. Nearly all its stages are marked by debility, and in the latter ones this is usually extreme. There is also a tendency to relapse; and the patient is never safe from a recurrence of the disease, under slight exciting causes, until his health and strength are fully re-established.

The causes of erysipelas are numerous, and often doubtful. When supervening on ordinary diseases, or when occurring as a primary disease, it is usually regarded as symptomatic of a debilitated or a bad constitution. It is one of the common sequelæ of exhausting surgical operations, and is frequently met with in the accident-wards of our larger hospitals.[1] Patients suffering from lacerated wounds of the scalp, particularly when much exhausted by loss of blood, or when the nervous system has been severely shaken, are especially liable to it.[2] The previous state of

---

[1] In crowded and ill-ventilated hospitals it sometimes *appears* to be contagious; but the question of its being so is still unsettled. It is more probable that impure, close air, is the true exciting cause here; and that 'contagion' has nothing whatever to do with it. The ward I was in was remarkably roomy, clean, and airy. Nevertheless I must not conceal the fact which I afterwards learned, that a patient had died of erysipelas, only a week or ten days before, in the same bed in which I was placed.

[2] So liable are lacerated wounds of the scalp to cause erysipelas, that military surgeons in sewing them up are careful to do so with the fewest number of stitches that will hold them together, in order to avoid additional irritation. An unnecessary stitch or two will sometimes bring on this disease.

Under the word 'scalp' I here include the movable skin and integuments of the whole head and immediately adjacent parts.

health and habits of life have also great influence here. It is hence that the first few days of cases of this kind are always critical, and watched with anxiety by the patient's medical attendants.

One of the peculiarities of erysipelas is, that the delirium accompanying it is usually of a quiet kind, in which the thoughts take their tone from the previous habits and mental bias of the patient, and are often occupied on subjects suggested by sounds that fall upon his ear. It is generally unaccompanied by audible expressions, and is of a remittent kind, though often continuing for many hours together. In general the thoughts of the patient may be temporarily recalled, at any time, to present subjects and a more or less collected state, by addressing him in an appropriate manner. He is also capable of occasionally doing the same himself by a strong effort of the will. Inarticulate sounds that strongly arrest his attention have also a similar effect, though they afterwards commonly furnish materials for fresh reveries. It is whilst the patient is apparently lying in a state of heavy sleep, lethargy, or coma, varied only by physical restlessness of which he is, perhaps, himself unconscious, that the mind is often the most busy and taking its wildest flights. Another peculiarity in which the delirium of erysipelas differs from that of ordinary fevers is, that the visions that then occupy the mind are remembered in the waking or conscious state, and generally permanently. In this respect it resembles ordinary dreaming in which the illusions are often so vivid and perfect as to be almost indelible. It was so in my case; and I have found it to be the same in other similar cases that have come under my notice. I shall give instances hereafter.

Erysipelas is a disease that is common to all ages, and to all ranks of society. It attacks the rich equally with the poor, the nobleman equally with the pauper. The vigorous and hardy workman or labourer often escapes its attacks, or grapples with them successfully, whilst the man of wealth and rank sinks under them. The reader will probably recollect that, within only the last few months, two European sovereigns and a royal prince have died of it.

This explanatory digression will enable many of my readers to understand more clearly the nature of my case, and the succeeding portions of my narrative.

My third day in a London hospital found me still further altered from the night on which I entered it; and each succeeding day increased the change. The gathering clouds and the impending storm were now bursting over me. The period of incubation had passed, and the expected disease was already come to aggravate and lengthen my future sufferings, and to increase the critical nature of my position. It was still in an incipient stage; but was passing to its full development with that inevitable haste and certainty that always mark its progress in such cases. I now felt conscious that the inferences I had drawn from the consideration of my previous symptoms were about to be realised; and I began to review the past, and to watch the future, with all the interest I was susceptible of feeling. In my lucid intervals my mind was now chiefly occupied in recalling all I had read and seen in connection with the subject, and in forming opinions on its probable treatment, and its future progress and consequences. I was fully aware of its malignant character, and of the high probability that, in my peculiar state, it would either rapidly prove fatal, or would leave me in a condition from which I should never rally, or from which my recovery would be slow and tedious. The impression amounted almost to conviction in my mind; but it did not disquiet me. I remembered the consoling promise "As thy days, so shall thy strength be;" and I put my trust in God, and inwardly prayed Him to "cast me not away from his presence, and to take not His holy spirit from me." And I seemed mentally to have received the answer, "I will help thee;" "My presence shall go with thee; I will give thee rest." And help and strength he gave me, and turned my wandering thoughts to realms of hope and bliss, and tranquil pleasures and adventures, which not merely alleviated my physical sufferings and often raised me superior to them, but carried me over the crisis and through the trials following it, to which I must otherwise have succumbed. He had also, in his mercy, taken away from me the dread of pain and death, and had endowed me with a degree of calmness, confidence, and mental impassivity in respect to worldly things and consequences, that saved me from one of the most fertile sources of anguish to the sick. Then, and often afterwards, I mentally exclaimed with the inspired bard of Israel, "Blessed be His holy name for ever!"

If I recollect aright, it was on this day that Mr. H——, the visiting surgeon, whose patient I was, first saw me. He continued to do so on every subsequent Saturday, Tuesday, and Thursday, during my stay in the hospital. On these occasions he usually shook me heartily by the hand or wrist, and with some kind and good humoured remark uttered sufficiently loud to arrest my attention, commenced his examination, and gave directions in my case. Mr. D——, the gentleman I have previously several times spoken of, also continued his attentions to me with unremitted kindness, until he left the hospital, an event which occurred some short time afterwards. Not only did he visit me at the usual hours during the day, but frequently besides. Even during the night I have discovered him bending in an observant attitude over me, as if listening to my feeble and hurried respiration. This I can distinctly remember was frequently the case during those critical nights which it was doubtful I should survive.

Other visitors I had now almost daily; chiefly medical men who knew me, or were attracted by the peculiarity of my case. On my friend Mr. R—— visiting me this day, I expressed my conviction to him that erysipelas, which I had told him the day before I thought was impending, had now actually set in; and I called his attention to the state of my head and scalp. He admitted it was "puffy;" but, no doubt actuated by a desire to avoid alarming me, said no more on the subject. A similar feeling seemed also to actuate the surgical staff of the hospital, for it was some time before any of them would allow that my head was "puffy," much less tumefied. The state I was in, was such, however, as to leave no doubt on the subject in my own mind, feeble as it then was. This suppression of the truth on their part was a mistaken act of kindness, and one which, in my case, was quite unnecessary.

My personal treatment at this period, and for some time afterwards, presented few novelties or incidents to interest the reader. Every morning, or early in the forenoon, my nurse came and washed me by means of a wad of soft cotton-wool.[1] After removing my bandages[2] and dressings, she cleansed the respective parts, as also other parts on which the discharged humours or blood had run. She then either

[1] The wads of cotton-wool so used are afterwards thrown away. A sponge is not employed for cleansing the wounds or sores of patients in such cases, or even for washing them, in order to avoid the risk of transferring disease to others. A supply of cotton-wool is constantly kept ready in each ward for the purpose.

[2] The bandages of fractures, dislocations, and other serious injuries, are only removed by the surgeons, or by the 'dressers' in their presence.

applied fresh bandages and dressings, or temporarily covered the parts; and, with the assistance of my wife, put me on clean linen, if it was required. The bed was next made or rearranged. This was commonly effected by lifting me from one side of it to the other, or by lifting me out of it for a short time. Being replaced on my back in bed, and the pillows, bed-clothes, &c., adjusted as comfortably as possible, I was left to myself until the morning visit of the house-surgeon with his staff, who comes round about this time.[1] On his arrival at my bedside, the temporary coverings of my injuries, &c., were removed, the parts carefully examined, and fresh dressings, &c., applied, and fresh instructions given to the nurse. The rollers or bandages that held the fractured ends of bone together, and my arm and hand in their places, as well as the parts they supported, were also carefully examined, and if displaced, loose, or dirty, replaced by others. At this time this was always done by Mr. D—— himself, assisted by one of the dressers and the nurse. For some of these purposes it was necessary to sit me up in bed. The length of time they occupied, though in reality only a few minutes, appeared to me an age; and, as hinted in a previous chapter, before they were finished, I was generally so exhausted and faint, as to be fast approaching unconsciousness. The relief that the assumption of the recumbent position gave me, may be hence imagined. My bed-clothes were also straightened and rearranged the last thing in the evening; and during the worst part of my

[1] The 'house-surgeon' and the chief 'assistant house-surgeon' are, de facto, those who have the entire charge and management of every surgical case. The visiting (non-resident) surgeons whose names appear in the list of officers as the 'surgeons' of the institution, merely examine and advise on the more serious or interesting cases; but otherwise seldom interfere with the treatment. They also perform the principal operations on the weekly 'operating-day.'

case, also in the night, or toward early morning, by the night-nurse who was then on duty.

My food at this time was entirely liquid. At first it consisted of tea, beef-tea, and eggs. Next chiefly of eggs beaten up with a little sherry, with a little beef-tea occasionally. These were at first given me by raising my head and placing the cup containing them to my lips, in the manner noticed in a previous chapter; afterwards, as I grew still weaker and more helpless, by means of a baby's 'feeding-boat,' by which they were poured into my mouth without raising me, or from the spout of which I sucked them. A few days later it was found necessary to replace or supplement the sherry with brandy, to prevent my sinking under the debility and exhaustion resulting from the joint action of the disease and injuries.

My medicine at this time was nearly as simple as my diet. It consisted chiefly of tonics and stimulants—bark, quinine, ammonia, saffron, &c. Fortunately my stomach and bowels preserved their integrity and continued regular. Indeed, they never failed me. Thus other medicine was rendered unnecessary, and much additional suffering and danger averted. Had it been otherwise, in all human probability, I should not have survived to write this narrative.

Reverting to my own state from the point at which I digressed, I may remark, that the worst portion of my hospital-life now commenced. The change that had come over me, and was still progressive, was alarming to all but myself. Every hour was increasing the danger and difficulty of my position; and as to whether I should survive the crisis none dared to speak with confidence. The result was doubtful. Very so! And this not simply because the results of all serious accidents and diseases are more or less so; but because there was a complication of circumstances

—severe injuries and nervous shock, extreme physical exhaustion, mental prostration, and a supervenient malignant disease, following a reduced state of health—all telling against me. It was a critical position which those that loved me most, felt the most, and feared to think on. As the day drew on, my mind seemed withdrawing itself more and more from the objective world, and, as it were, contracting itself within the narrow limits of the frail tenement that formed its habitation—just as a mollusc shrinks into its shell, or an animal retires to its retreat to hibernate. In its seclusion it began to luxuriate in a world of its own creation, present, past, and future, to an extent infinitely beyond that which had characterised its previous wanderings. At first these frolics of the imagination were disorderly and disconnected, fitful, changeful, and discursive, pointless, objectless. Time, however, gradually gave them connection and coherence, and accompanied them with seeming powers of observation, reflection, and speculation, and a persistence (if not interrupted) until the subject commenced, or the object in view, was carried out to its conclusion in the way that seemed necessary or desirable to my disordered mind. In cases of interruption the imagination frequently resumed the same subject, or revived the same scene, and continued its operations on it as before. There were a few subjects and scenes that more particularly haunted my mind at this period, and seemed to be especial favourites. From these dreams of untiring interest and beauty I was occasionally aroused by some one addressing me in an elevated tone, or with his mouth near my ear; or by sounds loud enough and strange enough to strongly arrest my attention. On such occasions the thoughts and visions of the world of fancy passed away, and my mind was recalled to present objects for a time. I then listened, and spoke intelligently though feebly; and perfectly understood what was said to me, so far as my imperfect hearing permitted me to catch the words. Then I would reflect and wander over the new point or topic thus introduced to my notice, and ruminate confusedly upon it until my thoughts rambled from it altogether, and again became absorbed in the dreams and visions to which delirium gave rise. In this state much of every day was now passed; and nearly the whole of every night, until five or six o'clock in the morning, when, from the restlessness and exhaustion before referred to, I sunk into a deep sleep, or into a state of coma resembling it.

My hearing was the only nobler sense now left me, and strange vagaries it began to play me. I had only one useful ear now, as I have already mentioned; and even this one had grown so dull, that to hear with it distinctly required my utmost attention, a difficulty which was further increased by its position next the pillow. The sounds, particularly unusual ones, that fell upon it, being imperfectly heard or confused, were consequently often misunderstood and as frequently mistaken for others entirely different. Thus I was continually connecting them with objects and transactions to which they did not belong, and my attention was continually drawn to subjects which were suggested by these mistakes. Indeed, they constantly acted as "prompters" to my thoughts and inferences, and gave the "cue," as an actor would say, to the flights of fancy and the 'castle-building in the air' that followed them. It was towards the evening of this day that these indications of delirum began to show themselves distinctly, and the night rendered them mature. On this evening, for the first time since my early hours in the hospital, I mistook sounds systematically, and rested and wandered on the suggestions which they raised, without at the time being conscious that I was merely dreaming or delirious. Hitherto this had not been the case; for there were frequently recurring intervals in which, as often happens in a day-dream, I had an obscure sense that I was dreaming, or awaking from a dream. The loss of this conscious distinction marks the progress of the disease. Now the draught of cold air from the partly-opened window above the head of my bed passed in my mind for a breeze blowing from the river, and the noisy clicking of the door-springs for the rattling of the windlasses of barges as they approached the wharf. I appeared suddenly to have made the discovery that the excavations for the new railway-bridge then constructing had brought the Thames close up to the walls of the hospital, and that the sounds just referred to, proceeded from barges constantly arriving and departing in connection with these works. The obscure sounds of loud talking, in like manner, convinced me that there was quarrelling, and even fighting, near me; and a few bars of a ballad hummed by a neighbouring patient, caused a complete opera or play to pass before my mind, which I mentally saw and heard with all the distinctness of reality. Night multiplied and intensified these illusions; and with each succeeding day and night, for some time, they grew in distinctness, variety, and duration. In the night, however, when the noise of the street had partially ceased, and all was quiet in the ward, their character and subjects changed; for then they entirely depended on the fertility of the imagination, influenced chiefly by the pre-existing bias of the mind before my accident. The exceptions occurred chiefly on those occasions on which some new unfortunate was brought in, or when the ravings of some patient labouring under 'delirium tremens' disturbed the usual stillness of the ward and arrested my attention. To some of the more curious scenes, speculations, and adventures, that occupied my mind at this period, I shall refer more fully further on.

The reader will doubtless now be prepared to hear that erysipelas, in a malignant and persistent form, was rapidly developed in my case, and kept me long fluctuating like "a pendulum between eternity and time." In another day or two my head, face, and throat, had acquired prodigious proportions, and had assumed the peculiar fiery tint characteristic of the disease. The wounds on the side of my face and throat now became doubly painful, whilst the silver-wire stitches that held my ear to my cheek gave me absolute torture. I would fain have torn them out, and the wound open, had I had sufficient strength and recklessness to do it. At my request, and to relieve my sufferings, Mr. D—— kindly cut and removed one or more of them, and subsequently the remainder; and this long before he would otherwise have done so. The consequences of their necessary removal I carry with me to this day, and shall bear them to my grave.[1] Soon a copious discharge began to flow from the surface of my head and face, particularly from the former, and to run down over the pillow and the upper part of my body, soaking everything. At first this discharge resembled water; but ultimately it acquired greater consistence and was like the white of egg. As it accumulated and dried on the surface of the skin, and on my linen, it became very annoying, and latterly offensive. Now it was that orders were given to remove my hair. I well remember the day on which this was done, and all the cir-

---

[1] I understood Mr. H—— on his next visit to say, that they had better have been left in longer; but had he seen me at the time, I think he would have thought differently. I am satisfied that independent of the torture they caused me, worse consequences would have ensued had they been left longer in the wounds.

cumstances connected with it. Soon after the morning visit of the surgeons, at which the order had been given, the "sister" of the ward came armed with her scissors, and, in as gentle a way as possible, performed the operation which was to leave me bald for many months to come. My poor wife who was present and assisted her, entreated her to spare a few locks on each side of my head; but all in vain. Her orders were imperative; and she explained how necessary it was in such a case that the whole of the hair should be removed. I bore it patiently and resignedly—I was often complimented for my patience and meek endurance whilst in the hospital. At last she grasped my beard, and the ruthless scissors were upon it. It was then only that I protested as forcibly as my feebleness would allow, and requested her to spare me that. Mrs. C—— interpreted my scarcely audible wishes to the 'sister,' and ultimately, between us, it was spared. This trifling circumstance, then viewed as an important one, now raises a smile whenever it recurs to my mind. After the scissors came an enormous 'dredger,' and soon my head, face, and throat, were embedded in a thick layer of flour. I was lastly 'done up' in ample layers of cotton-wool; and then, as I have since been told, presented quite a picturesque appearance. Visitors to the ward paused as they passed my bed, and took me for a victim of one of the numerous fires that had occurred in the metropolis shortly before that date. Henceforth, for some time, there was double washing and bandaging, with 'flouring,' daily.

By this time the swollen and extremely painful state of the right side of my head, face, and throat, extending far behind, compelled me to lie, not merely on my back, as hitherto, but with my neck twisted round to the left; as it was only on or toward the left side that I could bear the pressure of the pillows. Having, at the same time, only one leg and arm that I could move, it may be readily imagined that the sameness of the position in which I was compelled to lie, hour after hour, and day after day, caused me much additional annoyance and suffering, and ultimately became intolerable. One source of annoyance and pain to me, however, was shortly after this removed. I had at length attained considerable success in shuffling off the dressings on my leg and ankle, and the poor nurses renewed them in vain; a fact which, with the partial subsidence of inflammatory symptoms in the limb, led to a change of treatment. The torturing cold-water dressings, the oil-cloth on which the naked limb rested, and the iron-guard that covered it, were removed, and bandages of dry cotton-wool were substituted. O joyous release! O happy change! I cannot describe in words the relief which their removal gave me.[1]

I was now getting rapidly worse—daily, nay hourly, worse, as is always the case until the disease I was afflicted with has passed the crisis. But mark the goodness and mercy of an all-wise God. The delirium and coma which accompanied it, raised me during much of my time, as I have already said, superior to pain, and afforded me intellectual calm and enjoyment, which I even now sometimes look back upon with envy. It was chiefly towards early morning that my sufferings were sufficiently acute to rouse me from these reveries. It was then that the irksomeness of my long-continued and unvaried recumbent position ripened into a source of intermitting agony, that the smallest lump or inequality in the bed on which I lay seemed boring through my sensitive skin into my very flesh, and that the bed-clothes seemed to rest upon me like a superincumbent

---

[1] See *page* 31.

weight that almost crushed me. A few days later and the fabled bed of Procrustes could not have inflicted greater torture. But I shall revert to this again.

It was now that I began to look for the arrival of my wife in the morning with almost daily increasing interest and anxiety, and thus the minutes of suspense preceding it seemed lengthened into hours. If I fancied she was late, I imagined that something dreadful must have befallen her. Then followed enquiries of the nurse as to the time, and whether she was come; which, owing to the scarcely audible tone of my voice and the dulness of my hearing, were generally fruitless. And when at last she came almost breathless with haste, and I again heard her kind and gentle voice as she bent over me and took my hand in hers, what a cloud seemed lifted from my soul. Ah! moments these of joy during those long gloomy days—rays of sunlight peeping through the murky clouds that then hung over me. I could relate many incidents and say much in connection with these, her early visits to the hospital, did my space permit it. How during my more critical days, when she had left me the preceding night with a heavy heart and gloomy forebodings, she came anxiously rushing in, scarce daring to enquire about me as with palpitating heart she approached my bed. How on one of these mornings she met persons on the stairs bearing the 'shell' or coffin[1] containing the body of a recently deceased patient to the dead-house,[2] and that sudden dread then seized her mind that she was too late—too late! And now it was too that the nightly hour of parting began to fall more heavily upon

[1] In hospital-parlance, the "black box."
[2] The apartment to which the bodies of deceased patients are removed, and where they are kept until claimed by their friends, buried, or dissected.

me with each successive day. Whilst the dear devoted being that watched over me, like a ministering angel, during those drear winter-days was near me—near me amid the gloomy scenes and unwholesome atmosphere of a hospital-ward—I felt a sense of confidence and security which banished that of loneliness and isolation from my mind. But when the hour arrived for her to leave me, new feelings came over me, and I often felt lone and sad indeed. And the encouraging promises of Scripture, and the final prayer and blessing, then uttered in my ear—can I forget them? Never! They were deeply impressed on my mind at the time, ill and feeble as I was; but recent events have stereotyped them there in letters of enduring light and interest. Ah! well do I remember the words at parting on one of the nights to which this chapter more particularly refers—the words of hope and promise she repeated to me, to cheer and support me under the trials that afflicted me. "Fear thou not, for I am with thee; be not dismayed, for I am thy God; I will strengthen thee; yea, I will help thee; I will uphold thee with the right hand of my righteousness." "When thou liest down, thou shalt not be afraid; yea, thou shalt lie down, and thy sleep shall be sweet." "When thou passest through the waters, I will be with thee; and through the rivers, they shall not overflow thee; and when thou walkest through the fire, thou shalt not be burned." "A bruised reed shall he not break; and smoking flax, shall he not quench." "Put your trust in the Lord, a present help in time of trouble." "Who is he that shall harm you, if ye be followers of that which is good?" Alas! alas! that I shall never hear that gentle voice again!

I shall now endeavour to amuse the reader by briefly describing some of the trains of thought and sports of the imagination which occupied my mind during my hours of delirium and apparent sleep. I still remember them, and probably shall long continue to do so. Indeed, they often recur to my mind with the freshness of the "doings of yesterday." Strange and outré as these pen-and-ink sketches will probably appear to some of my readers, I can assure them that they differ from the originals only in their length and incompleteness, no language being sufficiently forcible and graphic to convey the absorbing interest, and the absolute semblance of truth and reality, which they then possessed.

CHAPTER VII.

Delirium — strange thoughts and fancies — interruptions — singular visitors — early morning — day.

"How quiet every thing appears. It must be night, very night. The world is still at last; hushed in sleep, I suppose. Busy man rests from his labours now. I am awake though. Yes! I am awake; for there that red coal glows, and there it stares at me through the gloom; always staring. All around is silence and repose. Perfect repose, such as must be within the grave. Then is beauty there, even though it be a charnel-house. Repose! tranquillity! attributes of beauty, if not beauty itself. The beauty-loving Greeks thought so, and idealised them in their sculptures. Keats is right:—

> 'A thing of beauty is a joy for ever.'

Yes! for ever! as infinite as space; as eternal as the human soul. Ah! poor hapless son of genius! Thy pilgrimage here was a short and fevered one; thy life alloyed by sad realities, and prematurely closed by human violence. Yet thou hadst thy dreams of love and beauty—bright sunny hours to cheer thee on thy way—guides to

> 'That heavenly portal,
> Which, to the earth-born spirit, is a vision
> Of beauty all unchanging, all immortal.'[1]

Thou lovedst the beautiful, sweet child of song, and revelled in

[1] E. H. Burrington. Vide *Note*, infrà.

it when the cold, unfeeling world would let thee. I love it too. Let—

> 'Thoughtless fools despise
> 'The things of earth which are the things of beauty;'[1]

I will not—cannot! O beauty, fair enchantress! There is magic in thy very name. Thy presence sheds a soft and holy light around us, that draws and binds us to thee. Man's cold, dull, busy world melts away before thee, and in thoughts of thee. Thy impress is eternal; present or past, eternal; for when thou perishest it is but in seeming; and when the eyes cease to behold thee, the mind still treasures thee in her recesses, and fancy re-creates thee. Thy protean charms fondled in the lap of memory, and warmed by the sportive caresses of imagination, reproduce themselves unaltered but in vesture. Then the past lives in the present. Then by-gone days return, and every thing and every scene on which thou hast rested reappear to be enjoyed again. Nothing of truth and beauty, spiritual or material, really dies. The bright, sweet flowers that fade, and seem to perish, spring forth again from the earth, and, kissed by the loving sun to his own tints, bloom afresh in renovated loveliness and fragrance.[2] The infant rises a cherub from the dying mother's side. The frail form exalted by intellect, virtue, and religion, passes through corruption only to meet the certain resurrection of eternal life, renewed in youth and beauty, to dwell in realms of uncreated light 'where God is truly known.' The hushed voice again bursts forth beyond the silence of the tomb, to join the choir of angels. It is the love of beauty guides the chisel of the sculptor, and the pencil of the painter. It

---

[1] "*The Beautiful*," a sweet poem by Mr. E. H. Burrington.
[2] "The loving sun
"Kissed them to his own tint, and left them so." (Ibid.)

is the love of beauty forms the inspiration of the poet—Homer, Virgil, Shakespeare, Dante, Milton, Akenside, Cowper, Burns, Tennyson. Yes! I could see to read them once, and almost worshipped them. That dear old Shakespeare I kept beneath my pillow. I see them now. There! there!"

"The ideal beauty of the Greeks! Ah! that is beauty deified, in which art surpasses nature, or nature is raised above herself. The Apollo Belvedere, the Venus de Medici, the Farnese Hercules, the Niobe, the Laocoon—Yes! there they are. They cannot be forgotten—never! Well! I suppose I must be dozing—dozing in the Valhalla. No! In the baths of Titus then, or somewhere else. I really must be, for I have lost them. There goes the last of them—the Venus. They are all gone now. The Bay of Naples—Vesuvius—Pompeii—Herculaneum—Rome—Carthage—how fast I travel! How pleasant every thing appears. Too fast! too fast! I wish railways were done away with, and steamers at the bottom of the sea—sent to Coventry, Jericho, anywhere, so away from me. Such speed confuses the view. It is really too bad. When I return to England, I'll present a petition to parliament, to put them down. Hush, beating heart! throbbing pulse be still! Your noise disturbs me. Hush! hark! I hear a sound so strange, so soft, 'there's nothing lives 'twixt it and silence.' Listen!—Mistaken; always mistaken. Nothing! No! that cannot be. Nothingness is not in nature. What is, must ever be. Annihilation would create a void, a vacuum. Nature abhors a vacuum. It cannot be. Aristophanes—no! Aristotle then, or Newton, or somebody else—I forget who—said so. It is all the same, it was said by somebody; and that mysterious somebody must know, I suppose; else why say it. *I* do not.

Hark! I heard it again. It must be thought, fancy, imagination, if I did not hear that strange sound again. I must clip 'imagination's airy wings,' and whip thought into regular habits. Mind, like school-boys, gets too fast sometimes for reason, and requires a birching as well as them. Cowper says—

> 'How swift is a glance of the mind!
> 'Compared to the speed of its flight,
> 'The tempest itself lags behind,
> 'And the swift-winged arrows of light.
> 'When I think of my own native place,
> 'In a moment I seem to be there'——

Ah! you did? did you! So do I. So on that point there is unity of feeling between us. That Cowper was a nice poet; a Christian poet. He teaches as well as interests one. Perhaps he availed himself of poetic license; but I feel he is right, quite right here."

"Again! again! What can that sound be? Now I *will* listen. 'Truth is strange; stranger than fiction.' I should like to find out the truth here. Pilate asked Christ 'What is truth?' but he did not wait for the reply—'He went out again unto the Jews.' Hark!—

> 'There's not a joy the world can give
> 'Like that it takes away,
> 'When the bloom of early thought declines
> 'In feeling's dull decay.
> ''Tis not on youth's fair cheek'——

How sweetly plaintive. That must be the pale nun in the corner singing. It is too misty for me to see her. Sad! poor thing, I dare say. Like the Eolian harp, sighing out her sorrow in music on the breeze that gives it birth. But listen! I hear another singer above me, high above me:—

> 'Where the bee sucks there lurk I;
> 'In cowslip-bells I dwell.'

That's strange now; but very pretty. How many singers —all solos. Well! I am in good company, since Mab is here. Other minstrels; hey?—

   * * * *
  * * * *

—————'And out a maid,
'Never departed more.'

Now really, Miss Ophelia, you forget yourself. I am ashamed of you, though the moon quarters to-day. I think:——"

"Oh! do leave me alone nurse. Just as I get comfortable you come and disturb me. Take it off, do! That cold water——"

"Drat your nonsense. You've kicked it off again. Us poor nurses have got enough to do, I think. If I puts it on as often as I am ordered, you'd make a pretty fuss, I s'pose."

"Take it off——"

"Hold your tongue, and go to sleep. There, do; that's best for you."

"The cold wa——"

"Take it off, indeed. That's good now."

(Night-nurse adjusts the bed-clothes, and exit. Fresh pain and rigors come on—cold intolerable.)

"Oh!——"

(The poor patient grins and abides it; but not without sundry efforts to shuffle off the odious dressing.)

"Well! cold water is plentiful and cheap, and seems in special favour here. I wonder whether they are trying to inure me to water before turning me out to sport with the sea-anemones and mermaids. At all events they do queer things here. I suppose that arises from the house being in queer-street. Ha! ha!"

"How dark it is again. No! not dark! It is not darkness. Gloom! mist! obscurity! That's it. How sweet it used to be to welcome the early morn, to gaze on the first beams of Phœbus as he burst forth from the far east. He forgets to come now. Oh! why does he stay away? Perhaps the horses of his chariot have grown tired from being six thousand years in harness, and he has stopped to bait them. Very probable; extremely likely. I wonder who is their groom. Hard work to fodder and dress those fiery steeds, I should think. The old blind minstrel, Milton, sung of light; and he sung well:—

> 'Hail! holy light, offspring of heaven first born—
> 'Bright effluence of bright essence increate.'

Flowers, flowers, tributes of regret cast by the broken spirit upon the grave of something gone and lost; too late loved and valued, though once scarcely thought of. Such is man! And that other bard[1] who sung of light—what does he say?—

> 'At thy approach nature erects her head,
> 'The smiling universe is glad:
> 'The drowsy earth and seas awake,
> 'And from thy beams new life and vigour take.'[2]

True! very true! Though not like the bold notes of him of paradise. I love the light as well as ye, bright sons of song. I always did. Who can dislike it? Who shun it?

> 'Imposture shrinks from light,
> 'And dreads the curious eye:'——

Ah! well it may; as do all those whose deeds are evil. But why does the light absent itself so long from me. ''Tis strange! 'tis passing strange!' I cannot unriddle it.'.'

"There is certainly a cockroach creeping up the wall.

[1] Yalden.   [2] Ode to light.

No! It is a death-watch tapping on the paper for its mate. How silly they make themselves; as if they had passions and feelings like ourselves. What nonsense. Why there is no paper here—no walls—nothing but myself. It must be a lunatic asylum—Bedlam, St. Luke's, Torrington Hall, or some such a place. I could not have mistaken the house, come through the wrong door, and got into the wrong bed surely; as the bride did at the Eagle-hotel, Niagara, whilst Marie and I stopped there. No! no! Such places must have walls, yet I cannot perceive any here. Well! I must wait till the sun rises, I suppose. Perhaps he will rise soon, as he has been a long time away. Then I shall know where I am. He has evidently got lazy lately, and must have overlaid himself. When did I see him last? When was it? I forget; quite forget, it is so long ago. But I will not trouble myself about it now. I daresay M—— can tell me. She is a perfect lucifer at casting light on dark subjects. I wish she was here. I wonder where she is. She is not here—that I am sure of."

"It gets darker certainly, instead of lighter. It is always gloom and silence, or silence and gloom here, just for diversity; for the same reason, I suppose, that Patrick said he dined on beef and potatoes one day, and potatoes and beef the next, for a change. A funny dog is Pat. That fellow has got more wit than discretion. Didn't Dickens touch up the 'Circumlocution Office' with his 'He wants to know, you know.' Ah! poor fellow, 'Passing away! passing away!' 'Quantum mutatus ab illo.' As the Greenwich pensioner said of the Navy, 'It a'nt what it was.' And so we all come to the same end. Life is only a race in which all struggle to be first. All ultimately reach the same goal. It is only a question of time. 'The battle is not always to the strong; nor the race to the swift.' At last comes death. Dead and forgotten—unpleasant words. Death cannot be a comfortable visitor to those unprepared for him. But there! few, very few pause and think in time. Serious matters not involving the almighty £ s. d. folks seem to trifle with, or neglect—one or the other. At all events they appear to think very little about them, if they think at all. The precipice is always before them— they know not how nigh—with a yawning gulf beyond it; yet they go rushing on and heed it not until—*too late!* Unexpected! too near! too soon! Yes! too soon for *them*. The Son of Man on his coming finds them unprepared—unprepared to meet him. 'Let him who thinketh he standeth take heed lest he fall.' Death is a serious affair that cannot be put off, or trifled with.—

> ' To die—to sleep—
> ' To sleep—perchance, to dream—ay, there's the rub—
> ' For in that sleep of death, what dreams may come,
> ' Must give us pause.'——
>
> *　　*　　*　　*　　*
>
> ' The dread of something after death,
> ' (That undiscovered country from whose bourn
> ' No traveller returns) puzzles the will.'
>
> *　　*　　*　　*　　*
>
> ' Thus conscience does make cowards of us all :'—

No! not all! Soaring on the cherub-wings of faith, no Christian fears to die; no Christian dreads futurity. 'Blessed are the pure in heart; for they shall see God.' Yes! walk with him in this world, and see and live with him in the next. 'When this corruptible shall have put on incorruption, and this mortal shall have put on immortality, then shall be brought to pass the saying that is written, Death is swallowed up in victory.' How foolish not to be prepared. 'The sting of death is sin.' Preparedness removes this sting, and insures the victory."

"I wonder when I shall die? and how? Ah! that knowledge is denied me; wisely, no doubt.—

> 'Shall death's harsh yoke
> 'Subdue me by a single stroke?
> 'Or shall my fainting form sustain
> 'The tedious languishing of pain,'
> 'As now;——
> 'Sinking in weariness away,
> 'Slowly and sadly, day by day?'

I long to know; truly long to know. Pause and think then. Yes! I'll think. Oh! I would think, but cannot. I get bewildered so. Something or other interrupts me. What is it? There! There! There is a shadow resting on me. The air seems all in motion. Mist! mist! I have it now. The place is haunted by bats. No!—rats—aerial rats. They must be rats. What other quadrupeds or bipeds would be capering about here in the still hours of night. How strange that no one before myself has noticed them here. The air is getting clearer now. Light! more light! I pray thee—'just enough light to render darkness visible.' There! that is better. There *is* a ceiling then above me. I am sure there is. And if a ceiling, there must be walls to bear it; unless, like the orbs in space, it is supported by nothing. There are strange things nowadays; but I cannot believe in ceilings without walls beneath them. No! no! There is certainly a huge beam stretching across above me. I can just descry its outline, and that is all. Yes! And there is a circular pole running along beneath it. A large tube, no doubt, with a slit or holes in its upper surface. It is a ventilator, I dare say. I wish I could get up to it, and decide the question."

"There! there they are again—those rats. What grim, rusty things they look, racing about as if they were at home.

I wonder why the folks here do not keep a dog or cat, just to catch them. No! no! 'That would be wrong,' I suppose they would say. Well, in saying that it would be wrong, they may be right. Why should man destroy what God has made? Why take away that life which he cannot give? He does though. Man delights in doing it. He is the most rapacious and bloodthirsty animal in all creation. The tiger is a lamb compared to him; and the vulture, a very dove. Nothing escapes his omnivorous jaws. Half creation bleeds to satisfy his appetite. Not enough! not enough! is his continual cry; and he seeks for more, and would sacrifice the whole. Unlike the prowling wolf, or bear, or lion, who pounces on his prey and then devours it, only when hunger bids it, man tries to create and keep alive his appetite by dainty cookery and condiments, so that he may glut himself and still have taste for more. His palate and his eye must both be pleased—two senses fed at once. The writhing cod is slashed, the poor patient calf doomed to a lingering death, the lobster boiled alive—all tortured—for him, and by him. What he cannot eat he hunts, shoots, angles for, baits, destroys, merely to gratify his thirst for blood and torture. Not enough for him! No! He must 'let loose the dogs of war,' strike and slay his brethren, and midst the carnage of the battle field, the sack of slaughtered cities—midst curses, rapine, groans, and death—raise the idol of his lust he miscalls glory, ere he is satisfied. But rats! we may destroy rats, I think. Certainly we may. Their destruction is necessary to our safety and comfort. Even my vegetarian friends do that. Yet see what happy creatures they appear, chasing each other, as if in pastime."

"How silly I am. I must have been dreaming. They were not rats I saw; or else the old revellers have decamped, and new ones come. I can scarcely see them through the sombre light; but they are not rats. I'll watch them nevertheless. They are of a dusky greenish grey, I think. That is better that the colour of their grim predecessors. What strange forms. They move so quickly that their precise outline escapes detection. Now they grow brighter, now fade into obscurity; now an eye beams forth light, now is lost to the view. Interesting creatures. I wish they would remain still, that I might examine them. How I should like to catch one for the purpose. I wonder where they retire during the day-time. Perhaps noise and daylight would destroy them. They are getting brighter. O, for light! more light! If the gloom and mist would clear away a little, I might discover their nature. See! they increase in number. What a multitude. Now they are more distinguishable. I know them now. They are the 'chameleon-lizards' described by Agassiz and Cuvier,[1] that are formed of zephyrs, and that feed on moonbeams. What beautiful creatures! what graceful forms; covered with iridescent scales of the softest hues, in which pale green and violet predominate. I can scarcely trace their tiny feet in their rapid movements. And what gentle, languishing eyes, that every now and then dart out rays of mellowed lustre as they pass. Oh! how kind to come and sport here, that I may see them. How they twist and twine, and chase each other, and dance in endless convolutions, forming the very lines which painters love. Now receding, now advancing, now darting off in tangents which, yielding to the attraction of the mazy circle, at last bend back upon themselves. On that dizzy pole, high in air, there they go; now 'on, on, quicker and faster;' now with lessened speed, in silent and

---

[1] Of course this was purely imaginary.

constantly recurring cycles. See! they never tire nor linger. On! on! through the long hours of night they never tire. Happy, sportive, beautiful creatures, may ye always keep me company. Does the dawn oppress you? Are you startled at the rising morn? Affrighted at the noise of busy life? Hushed be the voice of man then—stilled his chariot-wheels! Stay a little longer, bright ones! I pray you stay! * * * They are gone—all gone! I cannot perceive even one now."[2]

"Oh! that horrid dressing. Pain, pain! cruel pain! Oh! wretched bed! I am drowsy now; very drowsy. If I could only sleep. O, gentle sleep, 'tired nature's sweet restorer!' Art thou too frightened from me? Hast thou too ——."

"Nurse—nurse—do leave my leg alone. It's wet enough. I am sure it is."

"Did you speak?"

"Do leave me alone. Oh, do!"

"I'm doing your leg again. It's hours since I did it last; so you need not grumble. The dressing's beautiful! Is n't it? There! there now! That's nice, I knows."

"Oh! horrible!"

"There! go to sleep. That's best for you." (Exit.)

"That night-nurse will be the death of me, I know; with her cold-water what d'ye call 'ems. I am sure she will. I should like hot water better. If I had only my walking-stick or riding-whip here, I could push it off. A broom-handle would do. I'll invent and patent a pocket-instru-

---

[1] These delusions were undoubtedly suggested to the mind in the way noticed in Chap. X. The reflection of the wavering light of the large fire in the ward from the smooth, painted surface of the cross-bar alluded to above, and which was dimly perceived by me, was here the physical cause of them.

ment for surreptitiously removing dressings; so that a patient can buy one before coming here, and keep it in bed with him, unknown to any one. That is a good idea. I will plan one at once. Archimedes said, that if he had a lever long enough. and a place to rest it on, he could raise the world. We shall not want a very long lever here; and we have a place to rest it on; so those difficulties are settled. It must have folding joints, else that nurse will find it out. That is easily managed. I will now draw a sketch of it, and Mr. Weiss shall make it. I'll bring it to absolute perfection first, though. It must be made of vulcanite. That is light, and cannot be easily broken. Another good idea, that."

"How noisy the place is again. The street too! Yes! It is the street. Those cabs—those cabs—they go on wheels. That is evidently why they are so noisy. And the horses wear iron-shoes, instead of gutta-percha or India-rubber, as they do in Scotland.[1] How stupid of their masters. Vulcanised rubber will wear longer than iron. See how American goloshes wear. There ought to be an act of parliament to suppress noise as well as smoke—to put a ———."

"Oh! I must sleep. This mattress again—always hard and lumpy—not like my soft bed at home. Home! sweet home! shall I ever see thee again. Home!—the only word Englishmen uniformly pronounce correctly—there is music in it.—

     'How sweet,
  Under the covert of a cheerful home,
  'To clasp a faithful mistress to our breast,
  'And list to the pelting of the pitiless storm.'"

 * * * * *

---

[1] The "marsh-shoes" made of gutta-percha, and put on horses in

'(Sister loquitur.) "Well! how are you by this time? very bad, poor fellow! I see."

"Oh! very bad. I feel so strange—so——."

"Well, bear up. You will be better soon, I hope. Nurse is coming to attend to you" (at the same time pulling the clothes straight). "You must have your stuff you know."

"Keep yourself as quiet as possible." (Exit.)

"M——! M——! My poor M——! where are you? Are you come yet?—No! not yet! Too early—too early!"——

* * * * * * *

"My dear A——, it's morning. I am come again."

"O M——! my dear, good M——!"

"Do not disturb yourself, my dear A——. I'll get something for you; and then you shall tell me all about it. Do not disturb yourself now."

* * * * * * *

some parts of Scotland, to prevent them sinking into the soft ground, must have been thought of here.

CHAPTER VIII.

Nocturnal rambles — Aspen-dell — temple of silence — Stonehenge — Haldon-hill — Ide-vale — fairies' home, lives, pastime, history — elves — pre-adamite world — cock-crow — dawn.

"Now this *is* puzzling," I exclaimed to myself; "four cross-ways, and no means, in the gloom, of distinguishing the right one. It was a clear, starlight night when I set out; but now the air had grown too hazy for the stars to be seen. Well! the moon will rise soon, and though it be clouded, it will not be dark. How shall I manage? I am on the horns of a dilemma. I must trust to chance for once. Action is better than hesitation. Here is a stone. I will place it on the top of my stick, and then strike the stick on the ground. Whichever way the stone falls I will take. Done! That was a bright idea for such a dull night, I am sure. Not a bad one as the road turns out. Not a road. No! It is only a lane, with high overhanging hedges, and a tree here and there. That makes it so difficult to avoid the deep ruts. I must be careful not to fall into them and break my legs. How sweet the wildbriar and honeysuckles smell—quite delightful after the gas, smoke, and sewer-fumes, of London. They awaken pleasant memories of by-gone days. The glow-worms show their tiny lamps to assist me on my way. It is very kind of them. Nature *is* kind and beneficent to all her creatures None are too lowly for her care. Man alone, of all creation, is discontented and ungrateful. How shocking that seems. It is rather steep here certainly. Whither can it lead? Down into the valley, no doubt. There must be hills to form valleys. I am descending a hill now. I do not recollect ascending it. How still everything is. Not even the rustle of a leaf. The winds have forgottent themselves and are sunk in sleep. Perhaps they are now chained in the horrid cave described by Virgil. How absurd of them to bear it. Yet I am glad they do so. There is a light yonder; a faint, flickering light. Perhaps it's inside a cottage window where a fond mother nurses a sick child, or a faithful wife watches beside the couch of a dying husband. Ah! sickness! death! Serious matters though little heeded by those not visited by them. 'There goes another funeral,' says Smith to Jones, as they jostle together in the crowd on the pavement. 'That's nothing to me. Some poor wretch or other, I suppose;' replies Jones, and follows it up by asking the 'odds' on the favourite for the Derby. The death of one, or several, affects society no more than as many grains of sand washed from the sea-shore. The loss is felt only for a moment by their sister-grains they have supported in their respective places, and the next waive or gust of wind obliterates every trace of the microscopic gap. Now the light has disappeared. Will-o'-the-wisps playing for a few brief moments round the wych-elms—hey? Such is life! very much like it. Well! no matter! Let them enjoy themselves, poor evanescent things! Every dog has his day. Man has his short and fitful one. So let them have their minutes. Do not envy the ephemera, frail man; for thou art one of them."

"The way is clearer now. The hedges are gone, I declare. Quite open and pleasant; lighter too; and what light! So mellow and soothing, though little of it. The air! how clear and agreeable it has become. These grassy banks invite repose. I should like to rest here until the morning. No fairies or pixies[1] about, I suppose, to disturb one. No! no! Mere imaginary beings of northern mythology, hatched in the brains of the superstitious and romantic. They left this country when sentiment and chivalry departed in days long ago. And truth, honour, and religion, seem likely to follow them. This money-loving iron-age does not care about such things. No fear of fairies here, or fiends either. I will rest until awakened by the bright beams that 'ope the gates of day.'—

> 'Not to night! not to night!
> 'No sleep for thee till the morning light.'

"That's strange!" I exclaimed. "Very strange! I thought I was awake; but I must have been dreaming. The sounds seemed to come from the air above me, and near me. I suppose there is no one here worse than myself, as I appear to be the only being present. Solitude is charming sometimes; and this is solitude that Zimmerman would have luxuriated in. It is so grateful to the anguished heart and weary mind to be alone. I will, however, listen a few minutes before I yield myself up to Morpheus, the sleepy god. I will th—

> 'No sleep for thee till the sky-lark sings;
> 'We'll bear thee away on our azure wings.—
> 'Haste to the dell;
> 'Haste to the dell,
> 'Where the aspens grow,
> 'And the night-flowers blow.—
> 'There on mossy knolls we'll nectar sip,
> 'And ——'

---

[1] *Pixy*, an elf or fairy; a local word frequently heard among the rustic and lower classes of the west of England, particularly in Devonshire.

"So we will," I responded, interrupting the choristers; so we will if ever I get there; but I should like to taste that nectar you speak of, and have a quiet nap first. I am drowsy—drowsy;" at the same time rubbing my eyes to rouse myself. "So we will, if I do not forget it, and can find the way." I now perceived that the air above and around me was full of tiny little creatures possessing the most exquisite beauty and proportions, and floating on azure wings of wax-like gauze. They kept up a continued giggle and tuneful murmur among themselves, apparently of a most jovial character; whilst strains of soft Eolian music filled the air. "Lovely creatures!" I involuntarily exclaimed, "I will go wherever you will lead me. My heart palpitates with admiration of your beauty." I essayed to walk, but was not able to do so; and should have fallen had not some of my aërial visitors darted to my aid. I was then borne away by the united efforts of a number of them. The passage through fields of stilly air, occupying scarcely a minute, was delightful and soothing in the extreme, which, added to the soft music produced by the action of their wings, lulled me almost to sleep. I now found myself reclining on a mossy knoll, soft as down, and fragrant with nocturnal flowers. "Aspen-dell," shouted a thousand little voices. "Aspen-dell; hey?" I replied, "I wish I could see it clearly. I am so drowsy again, I can hardly keep my eyes open." "There!" said one of my new attendants, approaching me, and gently touching my upper eyelids with the tips of her tiny index fingers. "There! there! now behold! No grumbling here about sleepiness." I could now see clearly. The heaviness had left my eyelids, and the drowsiness quite passed of. The first object that met my view was the being who had just addressed me. I gazed at her bewildered by her presence.

She was the beau-idéal of female loveliness—a combination of beauty, grace, and vivacity, so pure, so chaste, so spirituelle, so fascinating, as to appear divinity itself. Her eyes were radiant sapphires; her crown, a wreath of gossamers set with star-like gems and flowers. Around her tripped and floated attendant graces scarcely less lovely than herself. I attempted to address her; but words failed me. I was so filled with admiration, so confused and surprised, that I stood gazing at her, like one lost, whilst shouts of merriment at my embarrassment arose on every side. I made another effort to speak; and was this time a little more successful. I now determined in my mind to pay my devotions at the shrine of the fair being before me; but my attempts to do so proved a lame affair, which provoked fresh shouts of laughter from the jovial crew around me. Then the queen and her court, with a gracious smile, passed from my presence. Disappointed and bewildered, I began to think of deferring my suit for the present, when a band of little choristers chanted in my ear " Look around! look around!" I obeyed; and how shall I describe the scene that met my eyes. " What calm beauty," I soliloquised. " It baffles description. Nothing in the 'Arabian Nights' equals this. Nothing but itself can rival it." On either side rose gracefully wooded hills to shelter and seclude it, lest the " winds of heaven might visit it too roughly." Here and there at pleasing distances stood aspen-trees of the most symmetrical growth—their leaves trembling noiselessly and perpetually at the ends of their long and slender foot-stalks, although there was not a breath of wind to stir them. Birds of the rarest plumage, known only to the witching hour of night, hopped sportively among their branches, coquetting with each other; whilst beneath them, at intervals, my interesting new acquaintances were gathered in bevies consulting or frolicking together, or dancing in mazy circles on the green sward around their trunks. Flowers filled the air with perfume. Through the centre of the dell a purling brook pursued its serpentine course, reflecting, in an endless diversity of forms, the various objects' on its brink. And light, celestial light, softer than that of the early dawn, and of the most delicate violet hue, illumined every thing. The gossamers floating in graceful undulations in the air, and hanging in equally graceful curves from tree to tree, glowed in it, like lines of pale iridescent sapphires, to delight the eye without fatiguing it. The very air—

——————————— "a pleasing stillness holds,
" Save where the beetle wheels his drony flight,
"Or drowsy tinklings lull the distant folds."

Such were a few only of the charms of Aspen-dell.

And now the queen, with her maids of honour and numerous retinue, again approached me. She seemed, if possible, even more beautiful than before. This time I was able to pay my respects to her with tolerable success. My thanks for her courtesy and condescension were warm and sincere, and graciously received. In return she created me a free citizen and knight of her vast empire, extending throughout the whole of these realms. The ceremony was a simple one. It consisted in laying her mimic sceptre across my shoulder as I knelt at her feet, and in addressing me by my newly acquired title as she bade me rise. A water-lily containing nectar, borne between the extended arms of two of her ministers of state, was then presented to me. After sipping its contents and inhaling its fragrance, my senses were exalted, and my heart bounded with delight. I could now see a thousand lovely objects that were before invisible, and hear a multitude of sweet sounds that were previously inaudible. I fancied that wings were beginning to grow out of my shoulders, and the sublimation of my material body had commenced. The ceremony being over, and the ministers of state departed, her majesty invited me to a seat beside her on a bank of flowers, and waving her attendants to retire, extended one of her gossamer-wings over my head, to keep off the dew. The tête-à-tête was a delightful one; and I might then probably have learned all about her realms and people, had I not been occupied in contemplating her beauty, instead of listening to her discourse. "Lead us not into temptation." Human nature is very weak. In an unlucky moment I forgot myself, and, throwing myself at her feet, endeavoured to kiss her hand. Then I felt the bud of a moss-rose that she carried, strike my cheek—a delightful salute; but, alas! the thorns beneath the bud also struck me, and proved less agreeable. Every rose has its thorn—every joy, its disappointment. Shouts of derisive laughter instantly rang through the air; and I heard the voice of my enchantress carolling out, at a little distance from me—

"For the present, good night!
"We shall meet again ere the dawn of light."

I started to my feet; but—alas! the vanity of human wishes—only in time to see the departure of the queen and her retinue, followed by whole troops of her subjects. I listened to the sound of their voices until it died away in the distance, and then started in the same direction. Here was an affair; but this was not all the misfortunes that fell suddenly upon me. With their departure the mellow violet-light died away, the dell and its beauties disappeared, and I found myself—I knew not where—with nothing but the light of the stars to guide me on my pilgrimage.

"I am getting tired;" I soon inwardly exclaimed. "I

wish I could sleep—rest—Yes! rest for ever. Life is but a fevered dream, that lasts from infancy to age, instead of for a single night. From this dream we awake only to die. Those who live longest, dream the most. 'The boy despises the infant; the man, the boy; the philosopher, both; and the Christian, all!' It is but dreaming. Poor child of clay! 'thy cloud of dignity is held from falling with so weak a wind, that it drops quickly' if death merely sets his finger on it. Ah! what is man? A breath at best, 'subject to all the skiey influences.' I should like to sleep once more—once more. I am happy—happy; but I want sleep. I wonder whether the Wandering Jew has read Shakespeare. If he has, no doubt he often exclaims with Henry IV.—

————————— 'O gentle sleep,
'Nature's soft nurse, how have I frighted thee,
'That thou no more wilt weigh my eyelids down,
'And steep my senses in forgetfulness.'

No sleep for him, according to tradition, until Christ comes to judge the world. There ought to be extradition treaties for the capture of tradition-mongers who set up traditions as truths and guides in place of Scripture—penal servitude to suppress such unholy practices. Scripture, without tradition, is my rule of faith."

"What a beautiful avenue I have just entered—rather gloomy though;—that is its only drawback. Cedars on either side—a grove of cedars; now, of cypresses—dark and gloomy trees; now of spreading yews—sepulchral and still darker, impressing silence on those who pass beneath them. Whither does it lead? Now it ends in an enormous open square, an outstretched plain of barren turf, on which nothing seems to live or wander. A very desert, so still that even one's pulse and breath are audible. I must go on—still on!" A huge building in the distance now grew perceptible; and a few minutes afterwards I was sufficiently near it to recognise its structure. It was of the most ancient style of heavy Egyptian architecture; and had a most sombre appearance. On approaching it closely I perceived this inscription carved in antique letters on its front:—

"TEMPLE of SILENCE."
"*The Sepulchre of All who Break its Stillness.*"

Impelled by a morbid curiosity I passed its gloomy portals. It was like entering some huge mausoleum, the air seemed so damp, cold, and heavy. Every step carried me into deeper shadows. At length I approached the altar at the farther end. Here ebon priestesses officiated in profound silence and solemn shade. Over the altar, in letters faintly luminous through the gloom, was inscribed—

"*Behind this Altar,*
in
Perpetual Darkness,
is the
Pavilion of the Goddess."
"*Some who enter its depths remain there;*
Others pass through them to Eternal Life."

On reading the inscription I was awe-struck. I attempted to retrace my steps. The darkness had become so intense that I was lost in perplexity. After groping about for some time I found the wall; and with this for a guide I hoped to be able to find the gates by which I had entered. In this I failed. Still I wandered on. I was now evidently in some subterranean labyrinth. "Shall I stay and rest here, or go on?" "Go on," something whispered in my ear; and on I went, with only the wall for my guide. How long I wandered I cannot tell. It seemed hours. At length I felt a pleasant breeze blowing in my face; and, a few minutes later, utterly exhausted, I emerged into the open air. On turning round to look at the place I had escaped from, I saw a board on the face of a huge arch of brickwork, on which was painted—" BOX TUNNEL.

G. W. R."

I sank down on the grass near me, and can recollect no more. When I recovered myself, I found I was on my journey westward.

* * * * * * *

" Salisbury Plain! Yes! this is Salisbury Plain, I know. It lies so bleak and open, so cold and cheerless—just as it did forty years ago when I crossed it before day-break on a morning in July. But there is no frost on the ground now, as there was then.[1] And those huge shapeless stones they call 'Stonehenge,' which we boys played truant to visit, and of which, the sight ill-repaid us for our tired legs and sore feet—is that here now? Gone! I suppose; like every other sacred relic of by-gone ages, to make room for some railway. Or, shorn of its antiquity and mystery by some modern would-be savant, or some critic on whom has fallen the mantle of Zoilus. 'It is still here,' did you say? Pray lead me to it. That it? Why it must have been rebuilt, or disclosed, like Pompeii and Herculaneum, by excavation. I always thought that those rough old stones were the mere fragments of the projecting chimney-tops of some enormous building below them, that had been buried by an earthquake, eruption, inundation, or something of the kind. I was right. Let us enter. How strange! The date on the sun-dial is 4102—Anno Mundi, of course. The fabric stands now as it did two thousand years ago. Even then the race that founded it was ancient. How

[1] This is a fact. On the night alluded to a very severe and destructive frost occurred, after a long period of hot weather; a very remarkable and unusual circumstance.

silent and dismal. Nothing changed here for nearly eighteen centuries. Lo! those prostrate forms arise. How strangely they are habited—like that Druid whose dress and learning excited the curiosity and admiration of ancient Rome. Not the brutal savages of school-book histories. Hark! The tongue is Keltic—pure Cymric—the language of our ancestors in pre-historic ages. Their calendar is more than fifteen centuries behind our own. Now the mystic rites begin. The sacred chant ascends. We must away—away! but whither? Alas!—

    ———' Like a man to double business bound,
   ' I stand in pause where I shall first begin,
   ' And both neglect.' "

    *   *   *   *   *

"How pleasant the sea-breeze is, as it kisses, in passing, the undulating plateau of Haldon. There is the sea—the English Channel—rolling its waves in the blue starlight. I hear them soughing and murmuring in the distance; and I see the white sails that bear the wandering mariners along."

   " 'Now I gain the mountain's brow;
   " ' What a landscape lies below!
   " ' No clouds, no vapours intervene,
   " ' To obscure the lovely scene.' "[1]

"Is it not beautiful? It awakens in my memory the oys of by-gone hours :—

   ' When on this spot, the evening still,
   ' At the fountain of a rill,
   ' Sate upon a flow'ry bed,
   ' With my hand beneath my head,
   ' My eyes have strayed o'er Isca's flood,
   ' Over mead, and over wood,
   ' From house to house, from hill to hill,
   ' Till contemplation had her fill.'[1]

---

[1] See *Note*, infrà.

'O happy hours of childhood, would ye could always last.'"

"Ah! there sleeps in stilly midnight old Isca's pride, a city that was founded before your modern Babylon. There reposes its venerable cathedral. There lie the ruins of old Rougemont—Cæsar's castle—the Saxon's palace:—

> ''Tis now the raven's bleak abode;
> ''Tis now the apartment of the toad;
> 'Concealed in ivy, moss, and weeds.
> * * * * *
> 'Whilst ever and anon there falls
> 'Huge heaps of hoary, mouldering walls.'
> * * * * *
> 'And see the rivers as they run,
> 'Through woods and meads'——;
>   Each town and village on their side,
>   Reflected in the murmuring tide;——
> 'Sometimes swiftly, sometimes slow;
> 'Wave succeeding wave they go
> 'A various journey to the deep,
> 'Like human life to endless sleep.'[1]

And there they end in that noble estuary, with the beacon hill of Exmouth towering high above its eastern shore; and with the railway twisting its unholy length in and out, like a serpent, amid the rocks on the opposite shore. And—

> 'See the mountain's southern side,
> 'Still the prospect opens wide;
> 'How close and small the hedges lie!
> 'What streaks of meadows cross the eye!
> 'And still the prospect wider spreads,
> 'Adds a thousand woods and meads,
> 'Still it widens, widens still,
> 'And sinks the newly risen hill;'
>   Distant harbours meet the view,
>   And cliffs for ever bold and new,

---

[1] See *Note*, infrà.

Whilst spires and hamlets rise between
Towns scattered o'er the quiet scene;
Further still the mountains rise,
And lose their summits in the skies.—

* * * * *

' Now, even now, my joys run high,
' As on the mountain turf I lie;
' While the wanton zephyr sings,
' And in the vale perfumes his wings.'—

* * * * *

' Ever charming, ever new,
' When will the landscape tire the view!
' The fountain's fall, the river's flow,
' The woody valleys warm and low;
' The woody summits, wild and high,
' Roughly rushing on the sky;
' The mossy seat, the ruined tower,
' The naked rock, the shady bower;
' The town and village, dome and farm,—
' Each give each a double charm,
' As pearls upon an Ethiop's arm.'[1]

"Dyer was a bel esprit, that's evident. I feel as he once felt. Here quiet reigns, and nature smiles in her loveliest mood; and peace casts her genial mantle over the sick and weary heart. I should like to remain here for ever—at least, for a season—a long season—till the doom of inevitable fate calls me hence.—

' Be full ye courts, be great who will,
' Search for peace with all your skill;
' Open wide the courtly door,
' Seek her on the marble floor;
' In vain ye search, she is not there;
' In vain ye search the domes of care!
' Grass and flowers Quiet treads,
' On the meads and mountain-heads,

---

[1] See *Note*, infrà.

> 'Along with pleasure close allied,
> 'Each by each other's side :'—
> And here beside the murmuring rill,
> The groves and knolls of Haldon Hill."[1]

"Peace, peace! Ah! man seeks it in the world, but finds it not. Satiated with the world's vanities and disappointments he shrinks back upon himself to mourn and maunder over those hours which his thoughtlessness and folly have for ever lost. And when to him 'time shall be no longer'—what then? Why his fellow-men chant over his remains, or engrave upon his tomb-stone or escutcheon, 'Requiescat in pace'—a beautiful prayer, only surely realised to those who deserve it. I am aweary of this fitful dream they call life—'tis but existence. Peace! peace! blessed peace be mine—be all;—peace that 'passeth understanding,' which the world can neither give nor take away. Such peace as our blessed Master promised to those that serve him. 'Peace I leave with you; my peace I give unto you. Not as the world giveth, give I unto you.' Be still then troubled heart! be still! This scene is peace, is solitude itself, now, during the watches of the night. It would be better though with some one to enjoy it with me—'with some kind spirit for my minister.' 'O, that the desert were my dwelling place,' is too Byronic for me at this moment. But there, Byron did not mean it; he only sung it. As he says—

> 'Feeling, in a poet, is the source
> 'Of others' feeling; but they are such liars,
> 'And take all colours, like the hands of dyers.'"[2]

"Well! 'who shall decide when doctors disagree.' I

---

[1] From Dyer's "*Grongar Hill*," slightly altered, with some additional lines which are printed without inverted commas before them.

[2] "*Don Juan*," canto iii., st. 87. Probably Dean Swift's sarcasm "Poets are liars by profession," suggested a like one to the mind of Byron.

can not. It is not all innocence and peace here, I see. Even here the hawk hovers and pursues his quarry, the weasel chases the timid coney, and the adder steals along the grassy bank to catch his prey."

"Why bless me, I have lost my way again. I have taken the wrong road. A clear case of 'aberration,' or wandering from the right path, just as a comet would do, were it to strike the earth. That would certainly cause a perturbation, and not give rest to perturbed spirits. I am going east, instead of west, as I intended. On the road to Ide, instead of to Ugbrook. It is a long way there—it seems a long way. It is gloomier on the side of the hill than it was on the top of it. That is natural. The high trees make it dark. Now I have lost the road—lost it altogether. I am truly 'faint and weary, a way-worn traveller, resting on the mountain-top.' No! not on the top—on the hill-side; and here I shall rest till the morning. 'Grass for my couch, and cowslips for my pillow.'"

*   *   *   *   *

"This is Ide-vale, I see. How I came here I do not know; for I fell asleep by the way. My fairy-friends must have borne me hither whilst I was sleeping. Lovely undulating meadows! There is the old church-tower on the other side of the vale; here are the brook, the hawthorn hedges, the grove—the same, the same as when I strayed here thirty years ago. Ah! those happy days 'auld lang syne,' when—

> 'The flowers sprang wanton to be prest,
> 'The birds sang love on every spray,'—

are past! long past! lost in the abyss of time, never to return. Ah! soft music fills the air. I know the sounds again. Here they come gaily tripping along—my merry little friends of Aspen-dell. I must mind my P's and

Q's this time, as I should like to know more about them."

My reflections were now interrupted by the arrival of the tiny beings before spoken of. I was soon conducted, with considerable ceremony, to the hollow of a moss-clad bank, at some little distance from the public footpath. Here, under the foliage of umbrageous oaks and elms, I found the queen and her court assembled. The recess was luminous with glow-worms, and the whole scene was filled with that soft, violet light, that I found always surrounds her. As my eyes grew accustomed to the light, I perceived all the beauties of Aspen-dell reproduced here, but in an exalted form. The very air breathed enchantment, and fascination hung on every thing around. Her majesty was very condescending and polite, and we were soon on excellent terms. The banquet was spread, and at once commenced. The queen sipped her nectar from a fresh-opened jessamine-flower, whilst mine was served in the larger cup of a water-lily. I found it delightfully refreshing and ethereal. As yet our interview had been chiefly formal; but now the queen and her attendant graces became more familiar in their deportment and conversation. She called my attention to the gambols of her little people in the pasture in which we were seated; and particularly to the cows grazing there, that every now and then started off alarmed, with tails erect, which seemed to cause them much merriment. Our tête-à-tête grew more interesting every minute; and I soon acquired sufficient boldness to ask her questions on various points connected with herself and nation. She replied very graciously to all my queries. Waving her attendants away, she seated herself beside me, rested one of her tiny arms upon my shoulder, and spread her corresponding wing over my head. This, as I afterwards learned from one of her maids of honour, was the greatest condescension, and the highest distinction, she was ever known to pay a guest. Her soft, etherial breath now fell upon and warmed my cheek, as she held her face near mine while we conversed together. A thrill passed through me as I felt it. I was almost lost in ecstacy; and was recalled to myself only by the honeyed tones of her voice falling on my ear. I assured her I was greatly interested in herself and people, and was extremely anxious to learn all I could about them. She graciously responded by telling me that she would gratify my wishes. In reply to my thanks, which were warmly expressed, she tapped my cheek with a rose-bud, and said "Listen then! listen!" I obeyed the gracious mandate, and thus became initiated in the mysteries and history of her strange race.

"You have very absurd notions of us in your busy, noisy world," she said, "and greatly misrepresent and slander us. Even the origin and meaning of the name which your ancestors gave us ages ago, you now dispute about.[1]

"Ah!" she continued, heaving a deep sigh fragrant as a zephyr fresh from a bed of roses, "Ah! We are not what we seem to be. Seemingness and truth are no longer wedded

---

[1] The derivation of the word '*fairy*' is uncertain. Lexicographers are quite "at sea" on the matter. Webster gives "Ger. *fee;* Fr. *fée,* whence *féer* to enchant, and *féerie,* a fairy" (or enchanted) "land," and hence also one who inhabits it. "It., *fata.*" He further remarks that "the origin is not obvious, and the radical letters uncertain. The conjectures of Baxter, Jamieson, and others, throw no satisfactory light on the subject." It seems probable, however, that the word is a corruption of the original, arising from confounding the sound with that of the Eng. word *fair,* an easy mistake and transition, when the reputed beauty of the fairies is taken into consideration. As popularly understood, the *fairies* are (imaginary) diminutive wandering spirits, that assume the human form, possess powers of enchantment, and amuse themselves by playing a variety of pranks on those that fall in their way.

sisters. We appear a merry little crew; but we have our sorrows and our bitter reminiscences. This western land of flowers and song is now my home—only my adopted home. In its grassy meads and mossy nooks I now hold my court. But we are ubiquitous, you must know. Spirits always are so. A wish, a thought, and we are there—any where within the confines of this cold, dull world; but we cannot pass beyond it. From evening twilight to the early dawn we enjoy this privilege. By day we lie concealed in the rifted trunks of trees, deep delved banks, or dark recesses of umbrageous groves. These are our prison-house by day—existence merely. The light is torture to us, and the relentless sun would slay us. I caught his beams one early morn, in the far east. Oh! horrid sight! The firmament seemed lighted up as with the conflagration of the world, the 'crack of doom,' the end of all things—that end which one day *must* come. The speed of my flight alone saved me. We can 'put a girdle round about the earth in forty minutes.' That beats your snail-like iron-horses, though they snort and roar so. They form one of the annoyances we fly from. We forsake the parts they penetrate for more quiet spots. Alas! they are now gradually intruding every where. If they come nearer I must close my court here, and retire I know not whither. That nectar you tasted?—"

"It was delicious; whence came it?"

"From the fresh-opened cups of blooming flowers—diluted with a dew-drop. Sip again!"

"And your food?—"

"Ambrosial honey from the same cups, before the bee has tasted it."

"And your raiment?—"

"The floating gossamers of summer's prime, woven in fairy-looms with rays plucked from the silver moonlight."

"How strange! How beautiful!"

"Strange, perhaps, to *you;* but not to us. You mortals stare and wonder at everything, and doubt all but your selfish selves. Abandon doubt and selfishness. They are the curse and burthens of your race. Hence your many-headed woes—your failures, disappointments—your——"

"Forgive me! I did not doubt you."

"Pray do not apologise. I do not blame *you*. I blame your race; and yet not them. Alas! 'tis their inheritance."

"'Tis not in mortals to command success."

"No, no! You are right; but surely it is a virtue to deserve it."

"And your nights—how are they passed?"

"In sportive play and merry gambols in the flowery meadows and the quiet dells, in al fresco concerts, in distant visits, in whispering hope to care-worn and despairing hearts, in suggesting pleasing thoughts and dreams to the fevered soul tossing on the beg of sickness, in raising before the desponding wife or mother fair visions of the absent loved ones—such are our pastimes."

"But are all your people so gay, so kind, so good?"

"Perhaps, not *all;* and yet I might say all. I will tell you. Long centuries back some of my people—the outcasts and pariahs of our race—rose in rebellion to dethrone their queen. I vanquished them. In solemn conclave with my privy council we banished them, and drove them from our presence. These wicked sprites are no longer fairies—they are '*elves*,' mischievous, wicked elves, and we disown them.[1]

---

[1] *Elf;* Sax. *ælf, elfenne,* a spirit; Welsh, *el,* a moving principle, a spirit; corresponding to the 'demon' of the Greeks. In popular language *elf* means the same as fairy. Shakespeare, however, seems to make a distinction between them :—

"Every elf, and fairy sprite,
"Hop as light as bird from briar."

They flee our presence. They delight in mischief. They are not fairies." (And she looked indignant.)

"Beautiful being!" at length I said, "There is *one* thing you have not told me. One thing I fain would know. Emboldened by your gracious condescension, may I dare to ask it?"

"Speak freely;" she replied, as she sportively tapped me on the forehead with the spire of variegated grass that formed her sceptre. "I will deny you nothing. Speak!"

"What are you? and whence are you?"

The smile on the lips of my fair enchantress suddenly disappeared; and I perceived, as she turned her head away from my face, that a tear, like a tiny dew-drop of rainbow-hues, was trickling from each of her eyes. I now repented having asked the question, and begged to be allowed to withdraw it; but she waved me to be silent. After wiping her eyes with a pinch of down gathered from the head of a thistle at her feet, she again rested on my shoulder. With saddened looks, which seemed to upbraid me for my curiosity, she commenced her reply.—

"The years of man's existence in this world form but a small portion of my long chronology. The sum of my remembrance embraces two thousand centuries. A long, long period—a past eternity to man's feeble reason; but only an hour, a moment, in the hands of God. Two thousand centuries ago this earth was like the flowery meads and pleasant groves before us, and around us, only more beautiful—much more beautiful.[1] There were no rugged rocks or mountains then to break its surface; no raging seas or oceans to lash its shores; no thunderbolts; no fierce volcanic fires to shake the firmament and scatter death around

---

[1] "One generation passeth away, and another cometh; but the earth abideth for ever." (Eccles., i, 4.)

them. Crystal rivers then rippled through its undulating plains, and crossed and embraced each other in graceful network. At their confluences they formed lakes studded with islands—homes of magic beauty. The ambient air was cloudless ether, so soft, so clear, so pure, the diamond would have seemed obscurity to its clearness. And light, mellow, holy light, rested on it, and illumined all things, and painted them with heavenly hues. The animals that roamed the land, and floated in the air and waters, were beautiful, gentle, docile creatures, that did not live by preying on each other, but fed on herbage, or the flowers, fruits, and seeds, upon its surface. And this fair and lovely world was peopled by a race of beings composed of elements so refined and spiritual, and gifted with such high endowments, that they were only one remove below the lowest grade of angels. Their dress, of rainbow hues, was extemporised by the light that fell on them. No toil, no care, was theirs. The air they lived in was subservient to them; and their feet or wings bore them, almost instantly, wherever they wished to be. With their breath they inhaled the food they lived on. Their drink was water. The juices of fruits and flowers were strong beverages which they only had recourse to on special occasions for enjoyment and entertainment. Death was unknown to them."

" And their language?—"

" That was soft and musical, and flowing as the notes of the Persian bulbul,[1] and yet expressive. Vowels and liquids were its only letters."

" How beautiful! It must have been softer than that ' bastard Latin,' the soft Italian."

" Such were these people. And the Almighty Father after their creation blessed them, and bade them to love

[1] The Persian nightingale.

one another, to obey the laws which he had given them, and to live in innocence, truth, and unity, that they might enjoy happiness in his approving smiles for ever. Intellectual observation, study, and intercourse, and works of love and kindness, formed their more serious recreations; and graceful sports, familiar conversation, and distant excursions, their lighter pastimes—they had no labour. The remainder of their time was spent in devotion and repose. There were no churches there. The whole earth was then the temple of God; and every heart was an altar from which ascended the incense of divine worship."

"Happy, innocent creatures!" I exclaimed, interrupting her, "That must have been the 'golden age' on earth, that the poets sing of."

"The 'golden age' it may be called, and truly; but alas! alas! it did not last long—not very long. Scarcely a thousand years had rolled away ere discontent and ingratitude, jealousy and rivalry, sprung up among them. Their primal innocence gradually became tarnished with vices. Brotherly love declined, and soon even the worship of their divine Creator was neglected. They no longer looked to their Great Father for his protection, and his blessing; and they offended him by their constant violation of his laws. Then he withdrew his protecting providence, and left them to themselves. For a short time they did not feel the loss. In their arrogance they boasted that they 'did not care'; that with their knowledge they could guide themselves. But this foolish boast soon cost them dear. Their course was downward — downward — and they fell——"

"What silly, wicked creatures. How ungrateful!"

"Yes! they fell under the anger of their Great Father who created them, and made them what they were."

"I suppose—

> "'Twere long to tell, and sad to trace,
> 'Each step from splendour to disgrace;'"

I remarked.

" 'Twere long, indeed. Enough! enough! I———;" and again a deep sigh was followed by tears.

"Beautiful angel!" I involuntarily exclaimed; "Tell me the rest, I pray you."

"I will, I will," she continued, "although the narrative pains me."

"Centuries passed away, and then that dread point in the great cycle of revolving worlds[1] was reached—it happens once in some twice ten thousand years—and———. But I dare not—scarcely dare to———"

"Go on, I pray of you. O, do go on!"

"The protecting arm of the Almighty Father having been withdrawn, the earth trembled perturbed, and all its beauty, with those upon it, perished."

"What? all that beautiful creation—those once happy beings—perished?"

"'The rivers forsook their beds, and the rush of warring winds and battling waves, mingled the land and waters together, or left them a mere foul and dreary marsh. One universal shriek arose—the requiem of departed life and loveliness. Then all was still again; and deep mists arose and veiled the face of heaven in perpetual gloom approaching darkness. Then chaos reigned for twice ten thousand years."

"And did all those lovely and once happy beings perish? —die?" I again asked.

"Countless millions perished—all the wicked—all who

---

[1] The great astronomical period of 22,000 years was probably thought of.

had forgotten God their Father, perished and met their everlasting doom."

" Horrible! most horrible!"

"Of material beings, certain tribes of molluscs alone permanently survived the fearful wreck; and these, attenuated by the enduring darkness of succeeding ages, dwindled down to the minute and microscopic forms found at the bottom of your ocean, and in your fossiliferous rocks."

" And did *none* of the strange people you have described survive the general doom?—*none?*"

"Only a few, a very few out of their vast number. A few less thoughtless and less wicked than the rest; and only some of these for any length of time."

" And how?—"

"They crept into the shells of the paper-nautilus[1]—those little arks still sometimes seen sailing on your seas and ocean. There they lay hidden, and floated until the catastrophe was passed. Then they rested on the dank grass of the cold, wet marshes; but not without their share of punishment."

" How so?—"

" The sins of the parents fell upon the offspring—it is one of the natural laws. It was decreed that, to them the night of the long ages following their fall should evermore unfit them for existence in the light of day, and that when it fell upon them it should destroy them. And this continues until now—even now."

"Impossible! Do I dream?—You would deceive me and amuse me with a fable."

---

[1] The *argonauta argo* of malacologists, popularly called the *paper-nautilus* or *Portuguese man-of-war*, is here alluded to. It has a boat-like shell in which it floats on the ocean in fine sunny weather, and erects its arms, like little sails, to catch the wind.

"No I do not. I would not do so. I speak of what I have seen. I will tell you more :—

"The little band of this 'strange people'—as you call them—that escaped destruction, still survive and live upon the earth. They still survive, though dwarfed by darkness, and shorn of half their intellect and beauty by the curse of sin that came to them by inheritance. Old they never get. They feel not age nor time whilst they exist. Existence and remembrance is now their lot—their punishment. They are a gay and merry lot by nature and descent; but half their frolics are to banish care and the memory of the past."

"After their fall—what then?"

"I have told you nearly all—all you could bear.

"After their fall they passed the long age of chaos. Then through those six long cycles of returning time which made up the periods[1] of the new creation ending in the Almighty Father forming man—not from ethereal essence, but from dust—that dust his sins have doomed him to return to. Obedience, love, and gratitude—trifles surely—were all he was to give in return to him who made him, and placed him in the paradise of Eden; and yet he failed and fell—like us—like us!"

"Like you! It cannot be!"

"Like us! Yes; like us! But hark! I hear the cock in yonder homestead crowing. I scent the approaching dawn. Away! away!"

A soft flutter of wings, and a few strains of aërial music followed the announcement made by the Queen. The glow-worms extinguished their tiny lamps, and all was silence and darkness once more.

[1] *Days.* The Hebrew word expresses either a day or a period. The latter is probably the sense intended to be conveyed in Genesis. This view is supported by the strong evidence afforded by geology and astronomy, and is now generally received by learned biblical critics.

"Where am I?" I exclaimed, as I rose cold and shivering, and damp with fallen dew. "Have I been dreaming? Was it a vision, or reality?" Puzzled and amazed, I staggered forward a few steps, and found myself treading on the soft sward of a luxuriant pasture. Gradually my eyes became accustomed to the gloom, and I was able to descry the dim outline of the old church-tower at some little distance before me; and I could hear the murmuring of the brook that ran between where I stood and the village. I determined to seek the public foot-path, and to return home by it. "It lies near me. I know it well. Ah! that good old path with its agreeable associations; and that quiet, shady lane, with its high, overhanging hedge-rows, in which the wild rose coquetted with the honeysuckle, and abashed the modest violet, primrose, and wild strawberry beneath them:—how pleasant they were wont to be!" I now bent my steps toward the foot-path, but was unable to find it. Then I changed my direction more than once; but with equal ill-success. I turned again toward that landmark, the old church-tower. I could not see it through the mist that had risen, as usual, with the early dawn. Long, long I wandered, this way and the other—across, around, in every direction memory or fancy suggested; but neither path, nor gate, nor hedge, could I find.[1] I grew weary, drowsy. At last, overcome with fatigue, I sunk exhausted on the grass, and fell asleep.

[1] This is what is called in the rural districts of Devonshire being "*pixy led.*" So strong is the belief in it there (though less so than formerly) and the influence of the imagination, that I have known persons at night take the wrong direction on roads they well knew, and pursue it for miles; and others, who have lost themselves suddenly in crossing a field, and who for hours have been unable to regain the path, or to discover the gate, or even the hedge.

CHAPTER IX.

Strange end of a day's excursion—the Gnomes—accidental interview—some account of them—pleasant company—adventures—Ishmàiah explains difficulties—Shòphan speaks on language—Anak discourses on philosophy, discovery, and the vanity of human greatness—lost writings—Zàdok reads—old house near Leicester-square—discovery of ancient MSS.—results, &c.

A DAY spent in 'botanising' and 'mineralising' was fast reaching its close when, fatigued by my rambles, and with an appetite sharpened by long fasting and exercise, I sat down to rest and regale myself. My seat was a large irregular block of stone, being one of many that had either fallen or been cut from the overhanging rocks behind me, and near me; and which appeared to have been worked, at some time or other, as a quarry. The date when this was so must, however, have been distant, as the surface was more or less covered with moss, and wild-flowers were springing from the crevices between the masses and among the scanty herbage beneath my feet. The sun had set gloriously in the western ocean. The extreme beauty of the scenery so interested me, and the refreshing breeze that had sprung up was so soothing to my feelings, that I lingered until the shades of evening began to close around me before I thought of resuming my route. I then replaced my knapsack between my shoulders, fastened on my belt, and reslung my flask and canteen in their respective places. I now stooped and picked up the hammer which I always carried in my rambles.[1] In endeavouring to attach it to my belt it slipped from my hand, and fell on a portion of naked rock beside me. The noise of its fall was returned with startling distinctness from the surface of the rocks behind me, and was repeated in a thousand echoes gradually dying away into silence. I stood surprised and interested at the discovery I had accidentally made. Soon my memory recalled the pretty fable that so pleased me in my boyhood, of that fair nymph, the daughter of Air and Tellus, who, for love of Narcissus, pined away into mere voice which is never heard unless the place of her retirement be intruded on. The stillness, beauty, and solitariness of this spot would, I thought, render it an appropriate abode for her. Night was now approaching fast. Already the twilight was passing into darkness. The general outline of the larger objects near me was all that was perceptible of them. I sat down again, and sunk into a reverie in which the events of the day, and those which had just happened, successively occupied my mind. There seemed to be some secret fascination about the place that had obliterated the thoughts of leaving it. After some time thus lost, I groped about and regained my hammer, and amused myself by reawakening the echoes, by striking it on the masses of stone around me. Then I extended my exploits to the solid wall of rock on my left hand, that being the one nearest me. Gradually I proceeded with my observations and experiments until I reached the portion of the quarry where the rocks were highest, being that just behind the spot on which I had been previously seated. As I approached this part I

---

[1] Mineralogists and geologists usually carry a small steel-hammer with them in their excursions.

found the echoes gradually lessen in force and distinctness; and soon afterwards the heaviest blows that I could give failed to call them forth. The sound of the blows had lost their previous sharpness; and at every repetition of them seemed to become deeper, as if the rock was hollow or less solid in that part. A little further and I gained the spot where the wall of rock was most dependent at its upper part. Here the sounds grew distinctly hollow and cavernous, and assumed such a peculiar character that my interest in them was greatly increased. I rested for a few moments, and then renewed my blows with redoubled energy. Then I fancied I felt a current of air issuing from the rock and striking my face. I ignited a fusee and held it to that part of the surface. By its feeble light I perceived there was a large crack or fissure running from the ground upwards. I held my ear to the opening, whilst I struck the rock above my head. I heard the sound of the blow reverberate as it would along the sides of a vault or cavern. I listened again. I could now hear an indistinct murmur, as of a distant running stream. It must be water passing through remote fissures of the rock. Presently the sounds grew louder and nearer. Now they resembled the hum of a cloud of insects; now the faint echo of distant voices; now of distant footfalls. I began to think how easily a fertile imagination and a fearful mind may mistake the common sounds of nature, indistinctly heard, for others of an alarming character. The sounds grew more and more audible. I now fancied I perceived an obscure gleam of light through the fissure at which I was standing. I watched it closely. It gradually became brighter, though intermitting; and resembled the distant reflection of some light still more distant. "The rock must contain a cavern," I thought; "perhaps one penetrating to the other side of the hill, and the light is that of the lamps of passing carriages, or of the neighbouring town." I now sat down on a stone near me, and again fell into a reverie. In a short time I was aroused by observing a bright streak of light suddenly burst forth and fall across the floor of the quarry beside me. At the same time I heard sounds as of feet and voices apparently within the rock. "It must be a smuggler's cave;" I said to myself. "However, I am quite safe. There is no entrance to it here, nor can there be for several hundred yards; and, if any, only in the direction behind it. I have the open fields and common before me, of which I know every inch. I am quite safe; nevertheless it is time to go home. I will give them a hearty rap before starting, just to surprise them." Suiting the action to the thought, I swung my hammer round my head and brought it, with all my force, against the upright rock before me. I distinctly heard the sound of the blow reverberate along the sides of the cavern. The clock in a distant steeple at the same moment struck twelve; and, O horrible! the ground I stood on trembled, and the rock I had struck tottered and opened; strange light burst upon my eyes, and sounds of a peculiar, sepulchral character fell upon my ears. Utterly amazed, I involuntarily gave one wild leap aside to avoid the expected falling masses, and the vengeance of those I thought I had disturbed. My foot encountered some obstacle that tripped me up, and I fell, utterly helpless, between two masses of rock.

A few seconds after my fall I endeavoured to collect my shattered senses, and then turned my attention to the busy scene that now occupied the spot on which I had so recently stood alone and confident. Fortunately I appeared to be unobserved where I lay; and I could not perceive that any search was being made for me. "What shall I do?" I asked myself. "Prudence is the better part of valour, they say. I will remain quiet, and act only as the circumstances that arise may dictate. I must watch them."

By slightly raising my head I was enabled to command a view of the whole face of the rock, as well as of the space immediately in front of it. The scene that met my eyes was a strange one; yet not so strange as some of those that followed it, and resulted from it. I perceived the last portion of a train of waggons emerging from the opening in the rock, as from a gateway. These waggons were covered with capacious painted tilts; and, in general appearance, resembled the better class of large stage-waggons formerly seen in England before railways were introduced. Each waggon was drawn by four powerful horses, in harness of which the mountings appeared to be formed of solid gold and silver. The pace at which they moved seemed a steady one of about four miles per hour. At the head of each pair of horses walked a waggoner. The countenance of these persons struck me as particularly grave and thoughtful. They wore large, long, old-fashioned great coats, which, being blown open by the wind, revealed a style of dress of a very antique character, and somewhat similar to that which formerly distinguished the Quakers. After the last waggon several individuals issued from the opening in a manner that indicated the haste of persons late. Among them was one who appeared superior to the rest, as he bore in his hand a long silver mace with which he appeared to direct the movements of the others. He struck the lower end of his mace on the ground, and the earth trembled. On a repetition of the blow, the wide aperture in the face of the rock closed, which then presented the same unbroken surface that it did in the early part of the evening. He next brushed his left hand briskly two or three times along the surface of his mace as he held it in the other, and immediately it emitted a lambent flame which cast an unearthly light on the objects around it. He held it toward the rock, as if to see that all was safe. Then he turned round, and with his arm extended, waved it horizontally in different directions, at the same time examining the floor of the quarry. Having thus occupied a few seconds, he appeared to be on the point of starting to overtake the train of waggons, when his eyes were suddenly directed to the spot where I lay. He hesitated a moment, and then stretched forth his mace toward me. The light of it fell upon my face. "Ho! ho!" he shouted, in a hollow voice, to those that had just left him. "Ho! ho! a mortal!" Then turning toward me, he muttered to himself, "Poor child of time! from dust he sprung—in dust he grovels—to dust he shall return." I was now surrounded by several of those who had last left the cavern. They endeavoured to lift me, without violence, from my hiding-place. When they had effected their purpose, they placed me on my legs, still holding me. I struggled to release myself; and in doing so, slipped and fell. In falling I struck my head against the corner of one of the masses of rock near me, and became insensible.

When I recovered my senses, I found myself reclining on a couch in one of the waggons which I had seen pass by me from the cavern. Its interior was filled with a subdued light, resembling that of summer-twilight, by which I could clearly perceive everything around me. There was a table near me, in the centre, covered with books and papers; and around the sides were seats with arms here and there. The whole interior, apart from the arched form of the ceiling, reminded me of one of the private saloon-carriages of a railway. I was not alone. Three or four persons of the kind already noticed, were there besides myself; and were engaged either in reading, or in conversing in an under tone. Presently I raised myself a little, and immediately two of those near me hastened to my assistance. Through their kind attentions, and taking some refreshing beverage that they gave me, I soon perfectly recovered from my mishap at the quarry. I felt, by the motion, that the vehicle I was in was moving forward, but in what direction I could not tell. I now began to enquire where I was, and to endeavour, by indirect questions, to ascertain something about those into whose hands I had fallen. I found my new companions rather reserved; and it was evident that they regarded me with some degree of suspicion. In a short time, however, we were on excellent terms, and they then answered my numerous questions frankly and politely. I soon found them to be very pleasant company. Their calmness and gravity, the serious and intellectual nature of their conversation, and the distinctness, smoothness, and rhythm of their language and delivery, quite interested me. The extent of their knowledge on almost every subject, and their antiquarian lore, was actually wonderful. My confidence in them was complete; and I only longed to become better acquainted with them. In this I was not disappointed. They introduced me to numberless scenes and adventures which were quite novel to me; and I learned from them many particulars respecting themselves, and ancient art and history, and other subjects, which I should otherwise have never heard of.

The beings to whom my recent adventure had introduced me, I was informed, were Gnomes — inhabitants of the inner parts of the earth, and the guardians of its mineral wealth.[1] To them is confided not merely the care and pre-

---

* *Gnome*, Gr. γνωμη. The gnomes, in Caballistic lore, are imagi-

servation of its metals and metallic ores, but also their distribution according to certain laws and regulations which, in remote ages, were laid down for their direction. During the daytime they constantly remain within the limits of their appointed dwelling-places, and only approach the surface of the earth after the evening twilight has passed away. Then it is that they visit other localities, and make their periodical surveys. The results of these are often of a most important nature, and not unfrequently lead to changes in the mineral character of particular spots and districts. The noble metals and gems chiefly occupy their attention ; and next those that follow them in commercial value or rarity. The baser and more abundant metals and their ores receive the least attention from them. The leading principles that appear to guide their actions are all of a conservative or benevolent character. Thus to prevent a too rapid diminution of the mineral wealth of the earth, either by consumption or waste, they lodge it in the remoter strata, or conceal it so as to render its discovery, and access to it, as uncertain and difficult as possible. To populate new countries they disclose to some lucky adventurers its auriferous deposits or beds of precious stones, by which millions of others are attracted to it, and the foundation of a future empire laid. For this purpose they sometimes raise the nobler metals from their veins, crush them to dust, and scatter it on the mountain torrents, when it is subsequently found amid the alluvial deposits and sand of the rivers and valleys below ; or they split the living rock asunder, and disclose the veins and nuggets in its bosom. In this way, I was told, the buried and imprisoned gold—which exists everywhere—was brought to light in our Australian colonies. In other places they

nary beings supposed to inhabit the inner parts of the earth, and to be the special guardians of its mines, quarries, &c.

direct the electro-chemical currents of the earth on the appropriate elements, and form them into gems and precious stones, which they then either carefully conceal, or convey to other places and superficially bury, as they deem advisable. Here to punish an ungrateful proprietary, or a degenerate and licentious people, they break the continuity of the veins of ore with long tracts of worthless rocks or débris, or by bringing the winged lightning from the heavens and fusing them, so that they sink to lower strata, and all traces of them are lost; or they daze the miners' eyes with mimic veins to throw them off the scent, until lost labour and capital, ending in despair, induce the abandonment of the undertaking. There, for like purposes, they open the flood-gates of subterranean streams and fill up the underground city with the rushing waters; or they let loose the malignant choke-damp to drive the busy workers from the mine, or the still more fatal fire-damp to remove, by one fell explosion, man and his labours from the scene. The removal of the mineral treasures of the earth from one locality to another, for one of the purposes just mentioned, also forms an occasional, but not an infrequent part of their duties.

It was on one of their journeys, undertaken for the object last referred to, that I first came in contact with the Gnomes; and I accompanied them on that one, and many others afterwards. The preparations for these journeys are conducted in the secret recesses of their subterranean habitations. It is there that the appropriate receptacles that form the bottoms of their waggons are loaded with the ponderous ore or metal, and the conduct of the journey pre-arranged. The horses are borrowed from the neighbouring pastures or common, and are dismissed for others, after an easy stage of ten or twelve miles. Their heads being then turned toward the place from which they started, they trot

gently back, and do not appear the least fatigued by
their midnight excursion. Indeed, the whole weight of
the metallic load and the living freight being compensated, before starting, by the action of powerful 'gravi-
tation pumps,' the weight to be actually drawn is only that
of the empty waggons; and the use of the horses is merely
to draw the waggons forward, as directed, in their course.
The harness which, like the waggons, is their own, is of a
very rich and antique character, as already noticed. It
possesses the peculiar property of invigorating the horses,
and of rendering them perfectly docile. Attached to each
waggon is a peculiar magneto-electrical apparatus, with con-
ductors from it extending the whole length of the team and
vehicle. By the action of these apparatus the whole train
may be instantly rendered invisible at the will of its con-
ductors. This is always done when human footsteps are
heard approaching them; as also in passing through towns
and villages. These nocturnal expeditions are conducted with
consummate skill and judgment, and the calculations on
which the arrangements of them are based are founded on
observations of the heavenly bodies. The time of starting on them is the noon of night; and the time of their
close, if they last so long, is immediately before the commencement of the early dawn. Precisely at this time they
either arrive at the termination of their journey, or at the end
of some stage in it at which they rest until the following midnight. The spot may be a disused mine or quarry, or a mass of
naked rock or strata on the side of a hill or mountain. On
reaching it, the captain of the train alights from the leading
vehicle, and waves his mace of office, or strikes it on the
rock, which then immediately opens, and the whole train
passes in. Another wave or blow of the mace and the
adamantine portals close, and every vestige of the recent

aperture is obliterated. Then commence the subterranean labours of this singular race, and which occupy them until noon is marked by the earth's magnetism on their curiously constructed dials. At this hour all labour ceases, and the remainder of the day is spent in intellectual study and recreation, of which conversation and mutual improvement form a leading part. The interval between the close of day and the last gleams of twilight is occupied in making calculations and preparations for the usual routine of the night.

"And how?" I asked in one of my interviews with this strange race, "how do you manage to keep yourself acquainted with all that passes in the upper world? You seem as au courant of its affairs and progress as if you were one of us."

"I will tell you," answered Ishmàiah, one of my newly-made acquaintances. "It is during the witching hours of night, when we have nothing else to engage us, that we obtain our knowledge of the affairs, discoveries, and learning of your people. It is then that we visit those great treasuries of knowledge, your public libraries, museums, and reading rooms, your workshops, factories, and arsenals; but in truth I must tell you we find very little that is new to learn there. Most of it is old, very old; indeed, ancient—re-discoveries, revivals of things long lost to your negligent and forgetful race, statements, opinions, arguments, and hypotheses exploded or confuted even before Adam fell into his dotage; poetry that seems but echoes of the antediluvian lyre; styles and objects of art and decoration reproduced from the models of the older Assyrians and the earlier Pharaohs; things discarded, obsolete, or venerable, even in the days of Solomon."[1]

"What you say is strange, truly strange; and not very flattering to the race which you call 'Mortals.'"

[1] See *Note* page 122, infrà.

"Perhaps not; but it is true. You asked me questions, and my words, which surprise you, are the only answers I can give to them. I could tell you more—much more, but I fear you could not bear it; and more still were not my tongue sealed by the Great Father whom we worship, and who placed us where we are entirely for the good of your race."

"You are kind, I am sure;" I replied. "I am really grateful to you; and not to you alone, but to all of you whom I have hitherto conversed with. May I ask 'how it is you know our language so perfectly, and also the many different languages of the various races among whom you and your people travel and sojourn?'"

"One of our seers will tell you, if he deems it prudent;" replied Ishmàiah.

Then Shòphan, who had hitherto been only a listener to our conversation, broke silence:—

"You spoke of languages, and of our knowledge of them. To answer your questions directly, would be to confuse you, and to leave your knowledge of the subject where it is at present. To make it plain to you I must go back to the earlier days of time, those prehistoric ages when all was virgin innocence and loveliness, and these eyes, now dim with centuries, beheld that paradise of Eden, alas! now only known to you from two or three brief pages in that sacred volume which your race so seldom read. Know then that God created all things perfect, and man the chief and paragon of them all. In the image of his maker he created him; and he breathed into his nostrils the essence of himself, the breath of life, that endowed him with an intelligent, immortal soul, knowing good from evil. Each living thing, according to its form and sphere of life, at once possessed the means of expressing its joy or pain, its desires and wants, and of communicating with its fellows by signs or sounds.

Man among the number; but he alone, owing to the superior formation of his organs, and intelligence to direct them, possessed the power of speech. At first it was of a simple kind, and limited to the expression of his sensuous wants and feelings. The steps of its advancement were, however, marked and rapid. 'The Lord God brought every fowl of the air and beast of the field unto Adam, to see what he would call them; and whatsoever Adam called them that was the name thereof.' These names were chiefly exclamatory words corresponding to the ideas which their appearance or motions raised in Adam's mind; and, in some cases, were imitations of the sounds or cries they uttered. Then came the creation and companionship of Eve, and with it the desire and necessity of communing with one another. Thought now became the parent of new words. The flexible vocal organs of man enabled him easily to express the leading conceptions of his mind, and the desires of his heart, in sounds that were intelligible to his species. Wishes, ideas, and sentiments, soon found utterance in words adapted to convey them; and thus the vocabulary of the happy inhabitants of Eden grew in compass daily, until it became sufficient for all the purposes of primeval life. Each fresh object or scene that met the eye brought with it an expression corresponding to the conception of it in the mind; and each new want or wish found a ready utterance in vocal sounds distinct from those already appropriated to others. At first these words were mostly monosyllabic, and the mere names of things; qualities being expressed by the variation of the tone in which they were uttered, and by movements of the hand or head. After a time they included the names of actions, motions, and existence, and the simpler abstract ideas and qualities, and suffered changes in form, or additions to their length, to modify their meanings. These were 'substantives,' the primitive roots of all languages. Soon another class of words arose, by slight variations of the existing ones, expressing being, doing, and suffering. These were 'verbs.' Then one substantive came to be placed in apposition to another, to qualify its meaning; and thus 'adjectives' were formed. From these, in process of time, arose all the other classes of words called, by your grammarians, 'parts of speech'; even those that are expressive of the nicest operations of the mind. Your older 'adverbs,' 'prepositions,' and 'conjunctions,' are mere corruptions, or abbreviations, of verbs or substantives now lost or disused. All words were originally borrowed from the objects of external perception, and all those which are not names, through the substantive."[1]

"The primary significant roots of the first complete language of the world—that of the primeval ages, and which continued to exist until shortly after the deluge—were purely vocal, consisting of only one and two vowels forming as many syllables. Others, were formed from them by the insertion of a vowel, or by prefixing or inserting a single liquid or soft consonant. From these simple radical elements, spreading out into almost endless variations and ramifications of letters significantly combined, arose all the words of the copious and mellifluous language which formed the only tongue of man during the first nineteen or twenty centuries of his existence. Could you hear it reproduced it would ravish you."

"The Noachian deluge rendered a single family, for a time, the sole depositary of the original language of the earth. It remained the only language until the confusion

---

[1] "All words, even those that are expressive of the nicest operations of our minds, were originally borrowed from the objects of external perception." (Horne Tooke.)

of tongues at Babel. It continued to increase in copiousness, and acquired its height of refinement in the plain of Shinar. The building of Babel led to its rapid decay and loss. 'The Lord said, Behold the people is one, and they have all one language. Let us go down, and there confound their language, that they may not understand one another's speech.' 'So the Lord scattered them abroad from thence upon the face of all the earth.' This punishment of 'confusion of tongues' the Almighty effected by striking the busy multitude of Babel with defective utterance similar to that called 'stammering' or 'stuttering' in modern times; so that only those that were affected with the like degree and form of the affliction, understood each other's language. One only out of every three or four escaped the scourge. Hence the 'dispersion,' and the formation of separate communities and nations. In this way gutturals, and some of the harder palatals and mutes, were introduced into the words then existing, with an entire change of their previous sounds and forms. The primary roots of these languages were thus also correspondingly changed, and their final vowels replaced by some harsher consonant, as seen now in the roots of the so-called Semitic languages. The few who had escaped the infliction formed a separate nation; but, after a time, contact and commerce with the others imported fresh consonants and foreign words into their language, which thus gradually lost its vowel and liquid character. It ultimately formed that great language of antiquity from which the whole of the Indo-European languages descended; a language which your philologists conjecture must have existed in some remote age of the world."[1]

---

[1] The *Aryan*, I suppose, must have been here thought of. The subject, however, is now involved in mystery; and its existence is a mere conjecture.

"And the grammatical forms and inflections of these languages—what of them?"

"The construction of the primeval language, in its highest state of refinement, was based on pure reason, and on the natural order of ideas as they arise in the mind. Its expressiveness was great, and its inflections varied and numerous, but all of a simple and self-interpreting character, such as would almost naturally occur to any one that used it. The first language formed out of it bore some resemblance in its forms and construction to that of some of the still-remaining tribes of North-American Indians, and to the sacred Sanscrit; and, more faintly, to the ancient Greek; but it was nearer perfection than any of them. The construction and grammar of the languages from which sprung the Semitic stock, were of a very simple kind, and their inflections few in number. They closely resembled those of the Chaldee, and of the Hebrew which is a later dialect of it; both of which are preserved in your books. They were all, at the first, mere dialects of each other. Your Keltic and Teutonic languages are as ancient in their origin as any of them."

"Your remarks refer only to these languages as spoken. I should like to hear something about their written forms and alphabets; if I may trespass so far upon your kindness."

"The first written words were the simplified outlines of the objects which they represented, with others of an ideographic character. Their use commenced at the beginning of the second century after the fall, and continued, with various improvements for another century, by which time the most complex ideas and descriptions might be accurately expressed in writing. In its general character the written language resembled your present Chinese; but it was much simpler, and more fluent. Then phonetic writing gradually superseded it. The latter was based on a simple and perfect alphabet of the spoken language; and by means of a few diacritical marks and accents that were easily understood, and which were afterwards introduced, it was capable of conveying every sound and form of expression used in speech. After the Noachian deluge the phonetic system of writing for a time declined, owing to the neglect of literature. After the 'dispersion' the original forms were either neglected altogether, or were more or less corrupted, and were soon lost to the multitude'; a knowledge of them and their use being only retained by the seers of the tribes. Then arose new alphabets of a more or less rude and imperfect character, to meet the supposed requirements of the dialects and languages that had sprung up after the 'dispersion.' This was general among the descendants of Japheth; but some of the descendants of Shem returned to ideographic writing, or a mixture of the two; whilst among some of the descendants of Ham arose the laborious system of hieroglyphics or picture-writing. The most ancient of these alphabets, as well as languages, was the old Chaldee, which is preserved to us in its dialect you call the Hebrew. The Samaritan, Syrian, Coptic, and Ethiopic, are of nearly equal antiquity. The alphabet adopted by the descendants of Japheth in the great parent of the Indo-European languages, was founded on the Coptic, and was the best and most comprehensive of them all. The scheme of the Sanscrit alphabet, and its combinations, was a later modification of that of this alphabet."

"You will now doubtless see that, from the original roots of all languages being essentially the same, and all languages being primarily the offsprings of others that preceded them, he who is a master of the earlier languages of the earth, and who knows the mutations and additions which they have suffered in the growth of the other languages, will find no difficulty in understanding the whole of them. Thus, to take the Romance languages as examples; with a knowledge of their habits—their fixed interchanges of certain letters, and their elision and insertion of others—are they not intelligible to one who knows the rustic Latin from which they sprung? Is not your current English most familiar to him who knows its Anglo-Saxon roots, and the ancient and modern languages from which it has imported thousands of its words? He who knows the roots and words of the great parent-languages has little trouble in recognising them in their modern progeny. This accounts for our understanding the languages of the various lands we live and travel in. The locality and climate, and the descent, history, and occupation of the people, tell us their tendencies and habits; and from these we at once infer the nature of their language—for the laws which govern the development of a language are of a universal character, and never vary where the circumstances are the same. We then have only to make a few enquiries of some of our people who reside, or have resided in the part, to be quite familiar with the language of it."

"The origin of language is perpetually occupying the attention of your sages, who dispute on the subject, but never settle it. Does not the caged bird, though taken when a fledgling from the nest and kept in solitude, sing the same sweet notes as his more happy brethren that haunt the grove? Where did he learn his song—his taste for melody? Who gave him the faculty and organs to give it voice? God the Creator gave them to his first parents. So with man. It is mind alone that makes the difference."

Then Anak, esteemed one of their greatest sages, spoke:—

"What you have just heard evidently surprises you. It is probably new and strange to you; but it is neither the one nor the other to us. We could tell you many things with which your race is unacquainted, or of which a few among you only even darkly dream. To us who, since the birth of man, have seen the origin and progress of all things, and their periodical fall and reproduction, there can be nothing absolutely new.

> ———'History, with all her volumes vast,
> 'Hath but one page.'

Like Time, its parent, it moves on in cycles, and thus, at intervals, repeats itself. Human excellence and greatness, at their best, are vanity and instability. Like the wild flowers of the field, they bloom but for a season, and then pass away; but others like them 'crop-out' again from their buried seed when the returning tide of circumstances calls them up. What have you that *you* call new, that is not old, very old, although you do not know it? Your oldest empires are but summer-growths—the period of their prime can scarcely count its centuries. There were others like them that preceded them—that flourished, fell, and passed away, even as they will do. Your arts were cultivated and reached perfection thousands of years before you dreamed of them; and even then they were mere revivals.[1] Your learning, science, and philosophy—so full of errors and hypotheses, twisted by cunning sophisters into seeming

[1] "The thing that hath been, is that which shall be; and that which is done is that which shall be done; and there is *no new thing under the sun*. Is there any thing whereof it may be said, 'See, this is new'? it hath been already of old time which was before us. There is no remembrance of former things; neither shall there be any remembrance of things that are to come with those that shall come after." (Eccles., i, 9—11.)

truth—are but the same. Your great discoveries, your wonderful inventions, of which you boast so proudly—what are they? Things that were known in the primeval ages, and then lost, but only for a time. Each great race of men that sought them afterwards, found them again, and believed them new, and lost them in their turn. Your written history, which you deem authentic, although it is mostly fable, embraces but two thousand years—scarcely one third of man's existence on the earth; and its earlier pages, how brief and incomplete. Even your tastes, your thoughts, are echoes from the distant waves of time. And your literature and books—I think I hear you say 'Ah! they are our own. There were none, or none but rude ones, in the earlier ages —those prehistoric periods which existed as long before the commencement of your era, as you live after it.' 'Certainly none' you will say, 'none before the great deluge.' You are wrong, my friend. I recollect these books when they were issued in the forms then used, which differed from your modern ones; but still they were books—books which were subsequently revised, enlarged, and reissued by their authors, and also subsequently re-edited and enriched with more recent knowledge by others, just as your modern ones are. Our great 'Central Library' still contains some of these gems of priceless worth; and a few others, nearly as old, exist in an imperfect state elsewhere, in secret repositories of antiquarian wealth known only to ourselves. Zàdok have you the library-catalogue? Read a few titles in the English:"—

(Zàdok reads:—)

'Traditionary Discourses of Cain on Conscience and Repentance;'

'Jubal On Music and Musical Instruments;'

'Tubal-Cain on Metallurgy;'

'Lyrics of Adah;'
'Songs of Zillah;'
'Narbothes On Agriculture and Landscape Gardening;'
'Jared On Consciousness and Memory;'
'Enoch's, Gratitude and Duty; an epic poem;'
'Methusaleh On Health, Beauty, and Longevity;'
'Lamech's Never too Late to Mend;'
'Norah's Lexicon of Roots, Words, and Synonyms;'
These are antediluvian authors;" said Anak, interrupting him. "Read a few titles of the earlier post-diluvial ones."—
(Zàdok reads again:—)
'Nimrod On the Arts of War and Venerie;'
'Asshur On Architecture;'
'Menes On Civil Engineering;'
'Eber On Etymology and Dialects;'
'Joseph On Hope, Obedience, and Retribution;'
'Shisrak On the Heavenly Bodies;'
'History of Egypt to the Death of Rameses or Sesostris;'
"That will do;" said Anak, again interrupting him. "You now see," continued Anak, again addressing me, "that your learning, discoveries, and books, are not so new as you thought them—only new to yourselves. They had prototypes even within the limits of your era; and, to go further back, ancient Egypt and Assyria knew and possessed them all in essence, though not in name. Thebes and Memphis, and Nineveh, were the seats of all your luxuries, and arts, and learning, with much and many others that you have not yet attained to. And even these were reproductions and revivals of what had already been and passed away. All human things are mutable and transient—
"Vanity of Vanities!' 'The Lord rebukes man for sin, and makes his beauty and greatness to consume away, like, as

it were, a garment fretted by the moth.' 'Every man is vanity!' 'Thou, O Lord, turnest man to destruction,' and 'where is he? A thousand years in thy sight is as yesterday, and passeth as a watch of the night.' 'As soon as thou scatterest them, they are even as a sleep; and fade away suddenly as the grass. In the morning it is green, and groweth up; in the evening it is cut down, dried up, and withered.'"

"True, true!" I exclaimed. "'Pulvis et umbra sumus.'"

My attention to Anak whilst he was speaking, and my ready acquiescence in all he said, appeared to please him greatly. He continued his discourse. Presently the index of the dial indicated the near approach of the early dawn, and all was bustle in the long train of vehicles in which I was travelling.

"I can say little more to you now;" said Anak, "but Shòphan and I will meet you again to-night, and disclose to you some of the lost literature of the early empires that succeeded the great deluge, now forgotten, or only known by name. This buried treasure which I refer to, lies in your modern Babylon. When the bell of your St. Paul's tolls twelve, we will go there. Then———"

The exertions of the preceding day, followed by a night spent in travelling and conversation, now began to tell upon me, and a sensation of overwhelming drowsiness came over me. I felt a refreshing breeze blowing in my face.[1] In vain I tried to keep awake. My eyelids closed against my will. I fell asleep, and heard no more. My last thoughts were on the impossibility of my attending to my daily duties if I passed my nights in the manner I have described; and

---

[1] This sensation, which occurred very often during my wanderings, was no doubt occasioned by the draught from the window near me becoming more perceptible.

this was accompanied with a dread that I should be unable to reach home before sleep would overcome me.

On awaking in the morning I found myself lying in my own bed in the accident-ward of the hospital, feverish and faint, and racked with pains of which I had had no perception for hours.

* * * *

"It is nearly midnight. I must repair to the appointed trysting-place. There! St. Paul's strikes twelve. I have reached it just in time. Here are my friends Shòphan and Anak waiting to receive me."

The place of meeting was the garden of an old house close to the back of the upper part of Princes-street, in the direction of Leicester-square. The house itself is a venerable pile which has been so often repaired and, in certain parts of it, renewed, that almost every known style of architecture has a representative there. It had been for centuries the abode of antiquarians and philologists, and was then occupied by one of the most distinguished book-worms of the day. Among the vulgar of the neighbourhood it has long had the reputation of being haunted; but some of the more knowing ones shake their heads and throw out dark hints of its having been the resort of certain Jacobites, and that it is now kept by a certain body of Jews, Papists, Moslems, Freemasons—the name of the party varying with the fancy of the relater—for their midnight fanatical orgies. It is, however, a dwelling-house. From its spacious rooms and rich old library it, perhaps, may more properly be termed a mansion. The chief source of its notoriety to the learned is, however, the several MSS. of great antiquity that have at different times been found there, when its walls and ground-plot have been invaded for the purpose of repairs and drainage. It was into this building that I was ushered by my friends, and then silently conducted to the old library. I was told that the tenant of the mansion and his two servants—its only occupants—had retired to rest; and that I might have undisturbed possession of the place for several hours.

The library, on my entering it, was in perfect darkness. Shòphan then caused a pale electric-light to issue from a crystal which he took from his pocket, and immediately the whole interior was perceptible. On a long table, amid piles of books and papers, stood three very antique pillar-lamps at equal distances apart. These Shòphan lighted with a touch of his crystal, and I then perceived, by the open books and papers on the table, that the place had been only recently left by the party who used it as a study. Anak now took me to a large closet concealed in the masonry of one of the buttresses that support the old gable on which the library rests, and there disclosed to me a vast pile of old MSS., scrolls of parchment, and papyri, obscured with dust, and apparently crumbling to pieces with age. The sickly mouldy odour evolved by them for a moment or two repulsed me, and I retired a few paces.

"In this pile," said Anak, "you will find treasures amply worth all the pains and penalties of searching for them." Then, thrusting forward his arm, he pulled out three or four of apparently the oldest of them, and took them to the table. After opening them he handed them to me, remarking "Now Shòphan and I must leave you; but we will meet you here again some other night."

I now examined the MSS. before me, and found they were ancient Greek ones, older by centuries than any of those already known; a fact which I inferred from their being written with only the sixteen alphabetic characters introduced by Cadmus into Greece. They were in a very dilapidated and imperfect state; but by means of a powerful reading-glass I was gradually able to trace out and read entire lines, with merely an obscure letter here and there. The ancient form of the characters, and the number of Keltic and Teutonic words which they contained, were the chief difficulties which I met with. How long I continued poring over these MSS. I cannot tell, I was so interested and absorbed in them. It must have been for some hours. At last the lamps began to burn dim from want of oil, and my eyes grew heavy. Sometimes I found myself even nodding over the MS. I was studying. Then I heard the sounds of a pail and scrubbing brush on the outer landing. "The servants must have risen and begun their morning duties;" I thought. Looking up at the shutters, I saw a dim streak of light passing through a crack in one of them. "O, heavens! Morning is approaching, the servants are about, and I am here. What shall I do? I cannot leave these precious treasures, nor can I get away. I am drowsy—sleepy. I shall be found here, a trespasser, asleep." My anxiety was intense. It, however, did not last long, as I fell asleep in the midst of it.

Late the next morning I was awakened by the noise around me, and found myself in bed as usual, and M—— sitting on the chair beside it. I perfectly recollected my night's adventures, and at first concluded that my friends Shòphan and Anak had come to my relief, and borne me home.

* * * * * *

These visits to the old house near Leicester-square were repeated nightly for some time; but generally I went alone. On one of my later visits my friends Shòphan and Anak again accompanied me, and revealed to me some secret recesses that contained literary remains that dated back to the patriarchal ages. Taking me to the basement floor of the building, Anak approached one of the massy walls there, and struck it with the wand he carried in his hand. It immediately opened and disclosed beneath it, deep in the foundation, a little recess or crypt, filled with strange things that looked like damp and mouldy folded maps. "These," said he, "are ancient books far older than any of the MSS. which you have seen here." Then stooping down he picked up three of them, which he handed to me. "Now," he continued, "take them to the library, and examine them; but mind that you replace them here before the dawn, as the aperture will then close. If you are too late to do so, secrete them in the old closet of the library."

On examining these ancient books I found they were formed of wide strips of prepared papyri, of enormous length, folded together after the manner adopted by the Chinese, with thick covers of the same material attached to the ends of them, to guard them when folded up and closed. The first one that I opened was in Chaldee; the second, which was in Hebrew, bore evidence of having been produced about the time of Abraham; the third was written in Ethiopic characters, and seemed of equal antiquity to the first one. The writing in all of them was scarcely legible, and here and there was entirely defaced or obliterated. It was the last one that chiefly engaged my attention; and over it I lingered, night after night, until I had mastered some of its columns. On almost every occasion I suffered the same annoyance from the failing lamps, the approaching busy housemaid, and the final drowsiness and sleep. All, however, went on well for a time; but, alas! a sudden misadventure brought at once my visits, and my researches, to a close. I had lain back unconsciously in the easy-chair in which I sat, with my favourite Ethiopic MS.

in my hand, and had fallen into a doze. I heard the noise of the busy housemaid, as before, drawing nearer and nearer to me; but I was unable to arouse myself. What was unusual with her, she came my way with her pail and brush. She might have passed me unheeded had she not stumbled over my extended legs. The sudden splash of cold water on my feet aroused me completely. I instantly started up, and came into rude contact with the domestic who had so often been a source of annoyance to me. A succession of piercing screams followed, and the whole house was awakened, and at once in an uproar. I can recollect no more. How I got out of the scrape I cannot tell; but two things I well remember—I neither saw my ancient friends, the Gnomes, nor visited the old house near Leicester-square, again.

CHAPTER X.

The soul, mind, memory, imagination—sleep—death, futurity—dreams—somnambulism, somniloquism—delirium—my wanderings—operas—Cotters of the Rhine—balloon-excursion round the world—voyage of the yacht Daphne—discoveries—north-west passage—polar sea—second voyage—antarctic continent, sea, and archipelago—ancient MSS.—universal alphabet and language—extemporaneous houses—shifting of beds—restlessness, cold, sleep.

How incomprehensible is the nature of the *human soul* to man. Scripture, faith, and reason, tell us that it exists, that it possesses distinct individuality, and is rational, responsible, and immortal, and our innate feelings and desires prompt us to the same conclusions; but beyond this all is obscurity and conjecture.

And that manifestation or development of the soul which we call the *mind*, arising from its connection with the body, and the only one of which we are personally cognizant—how little do we know about it! The sum of our knowledge of it is derived from observing, classifying, and analysing its operations, matters so difficult that, although the subject has engaged the attention of the wisest of our race from remote antiquity to the present time, little or no real progress has been made in it. The how? and the why? of thought and reason elude investigation altogether. We know that the mind depends on the existence and integrity of certain material organs, and that it receives its impressions through those 'five gateways of knowledge' which we call the senses. We know the vastness of its comprehension, the multiplicity and variety of its conceptions, the beauty of some of its productions, the profoundness of its researches, its continual activity, and its enduring powers of labour. We know that it may be enlarged and energised by proper training; that it may be more or less suspended either temporarily or permanently, and even wholly destroyed; that it may be excited or depressed, or its operations deranged, by a variety of causes familiar to every one, and by others which, to us, are unaccountable. We know that it varies in power and brilliancy, and in character, in different individuals; and that even in the same individual it often fluctuates without assignable cause; and that it grows in vigour with maturity, and fails with the body in the decline of life. Beyond this, what do we know? Little, very little!

Then that faculty of the mind which we call *memory*—what do we know of that? Physiology shows us that its seat is the cineritious cortical matter of the brain; and that when either that or the primitive nerves of the cerebrum are removed, or become diminished or diseased, memory disappears, or becomes defective. We know that things are remembered in proportion to the strength and vividness of the first impression; and that this strength and vividness corresponds to the degree of attention or intentness with which the mind regards them at the time. We know that ideas do not enter the mind singly, but in pairs, and that ideas, either analogous or opposite, which have been once associated recall each other on the recurrence of either of them. We know that impressions received through the sense of 'sight' are usually much stronger and more vivid than those received through the other senses; that the 'ear' follows the eye in this respect; and that the strongest possible impressions are received through the combined action of these senses. In other words, what arrests the eye is, in general, longer and more clearly remembered than what arrests the ear; and that impressions received through both of them, are more permanent and vivid than those received through either singly.[1] But these facts do not explain either the nature or origin of memory; and so we content ourselves by applying a convenient term to the power the mind possesses of receiving impressions or ideas and reproducing them unchanged, or exactly in the form in which they have previously existed in the mind, without really knowing anything further of importance on the subject. In like manner we employ the term *imagination* to express an allied faculty of the mind that reproduces ideas in a form more or less changed, or interwoven with each other.

Sleep, "that knits up the ravelled sleeve of care," is another mystery connected with our being which has hitherto eluded investigation into its cause and nature. What is it? What is the state and relation of the soul, the mind, the body, during it? by what innate law does its mantle—that 'seeming death'—fall upon us with a periodicity as remarkable as it is familiar to us? We can describe the apparent state of the sleeper, the effects produced by sleep, and its object; and we can generally induce it by the administration of hypnotics; but this is nearly all we can do—nearly all we really know about it. We know that in ordinary healthy sleep the voluntary muscles, for the most

---

[1] It is thus that in a first trip by steam-boat from London to Richmond, or to Gravesend, every object of interest on the banks of the river may be readily recalled to the mind afterwards; a thing that cannot be done after listening, even attentively, to a description of them. The same applies to visits to exhibitions, picture-galleries, &c. Hence also the value of pictorial illustrations in elementary or descriptive works; particularly in those intended for children and youth.

part, remain inactive; whilst the involuntary muscles on which depend the continuation of the functions of life retain their full activity—they never sleep. We know that the senses close or fall asleep one after the other, beginning with 'sight,' and that 'hearing' and 'touch' are the last to do so. That in perfectly sound sleep all of them are closed, and communication between the soul or mind and the objective world entirely cut off. We know that both the mind and body exhausted by the labour, or the duration of the waking hours of the day, naturally seek sleep at some early hour of the night; and that on awaking in the morning they appear refreshed and invigorated, and ready for another day's toil or watching. We know that the functions of nutrition, reparation, and growth, are most active during sleep. We know that sleep is seldom so complete that some sense, some faculties, some voluntary muscles, are not awake. Indeed, persons are often half asleep when they appear to be awake, and half awake when they appear to be asleep, rendering 'waking' and 'sleeping' rather relative than absolute terms. Hence it has been asserted by a recent authority, and apparently with truth, that few of us are ever completely awake, or completely asleep. Of such facts and observations as these, which leave the primary questions unsolved, consists nearly all our knowledge of the subject. The rest that is said about it is, for the most part, mere hypothesis and conjecture.

Death, that final sleep to which we all must soon come—is it not as strange and mysterious as our generation and our birth?

"How wonderful is death!—
"Death and his brother sleep:—
"One pale as yonder waning moon,
"With lips of lurid blue;
"The other rosy as the morn,
"When throned on ocean's wave

"He smileth o'er the world;—
"Yet both so passing wonderful!"

And *futurity*—is it not shrouded in impenetrable darkness?—

"When coldness wraps this suffering clay,
"Ah, whither strays the immortal mind?—
"It cannot die, it cannot stay,
"But leaves its darkened dust behind."

*   *   *   *   *

"In darkness spoke Athena's wisest son,[1]
" 'All that we know, is, nothing can be known:'
"Yet doubting pagans dreamed of bliss to come—
"Of peace upon the shores of Acheron.
' 'Tis ours, as holiest men have deemed, to see
"A land of souls beyond that sable shore,
"To shame the doctrine of the Sadducee
"And sophists, madly vain of dubious lore:—
"How sweet 'twill be in concert to adore
"With those who made our mortal labours light!
"To hear each voice we feared to hear no more—
"Of Christian martyrs, prophets gone before!—
"Behold each mighty shade revealed to sight,
"The Bactrian,[2] Samian sage,[3] and all who taught the right!"

We are acquainted with the physical signs and nature of death; and happily we know, from revelation, that "this corruptible shall put on incorruption, and this mortal shall put on immortality."—

"Thou art immortal;—so am I: I feel—
"I feel my immortality o'ersweep
"All pains, all tears, all time, all fears, and peal,
"Like the eternal thunders of the deep,
"Into my ears this truth—'Thou liv'st for ever!' "—

But in what state? Faith furnishes a reply to the dying Christian; conscience, to the dying sinner. It has been

[1] Socrates.   [2] Zoroaster.   [3] Pythagoras.

truly said, that "The veil that covers futurity," both in time and in eternity, "is woven by the hand of mercy."[1]

[1] Much has been written on the subject of physical death, and particularly on the 'agony' preceding and accompanying it. My opportunities of observation have been numerous, and the conclusions I have drawn accord with those of Hufeland, and other German physiologists. I infer that the physical agonies of the dying are, in general, or at least very often, more apparent than real. I have the words of the dying to confirm my opinion. In a very recent case, I several times asked a dying patient convulsed and writhing in apparent agony, 'what pain was felt? and where?' and obtained in a feeble, protracted, but clearly audible tone, as I leaned over the bed, the answer "No pain! no pain! but—." I understood the omitted portion of the sentence to imply 'such restlessness and faintness.' I think it may be fairly assumed that all the sufferings that precede and accompany certain forms of death, as those by violence, for instance, are completed when insensibility sets in; and that a person resuscitated from such a state by surgical or other means, has physically suffered all that he would suffer were he left alone and actual death ensued. This is especially marked in cases of gunshot wounds, blows and falls on the head, and in drowning and other forms of suffocation. I think that I passed through, in two instances, all the physical suffering I should have experienced, had I not been resuscitated. The one arose from my horse falling under me; the other, from drowning. A full account of the latter appeared in one of the periodicals of the time, and an extract from this report was reprinted in one of my works a few years since. As it may interest the reader I will give him a portion of the last:—"After a few vain struggles, he (the author) sunk utterly helpless and exhausted. The recollection of a comrade that was drowned a few days before, near the spot, and the conviction of inevitable death, instantly flashed across his mind like an electric shock. Life, death, eternity—the dread of leaving his friends in ignorance of his fate—and a thousand other subjects, were idealised in a moment, and were followed by others in incessant and rapid succession. Space and time seemed annihilated—they presented no visible horizon to the mind's eye,—all was present,—all the events and actions of his past life seemed collected and performing at the same moment, as in a day-dream, where individual distinctness is blended with general confusion. A pleasing state of mental serenity ensued; the prospect gradually changed, and surrounding space seemed covered with verdure of the softest green, and illuminated with green light of the most subdued

Reverting to sleep:—In sleep come *dreams*. What is dreaming? Yet another mystery; or at least a state which the highest authorities have attempted to explain in very

and soothing tone, which gradually faded into twilight, and—here consciousness ceased. During the whole of this time, which occupied about 3¼ minutes, or, at the most, 4 minutes, no great bodily suffering was experienced; after the first sensations of suffocation were passed, none at all are recollected to have been felt. The feelings in the later moments of consciousness, indeed approached, in delectable serenity, those of the opium-eater in the earlier periods of his devotion to that drug. A quarter of a century (now one-third of a century) has nearly elapsed since the occurrence of the accident alluded to; but though time has erased from the memory of the writer many events of more recent date, and, with a busy hand, has scattered trials and afflictions in his path, yet the incidents that occurred on that almost fatal morning, still occasionally start up before his mind as distinctly as the doings of yesterday." (Cooley's " *Cyclopædia*," 3rd ed., p. 344.) About twenty years after this paragraph was written, I came across Dr. Wollaston's description of his feelings on the occasion of a similar accident; and was particularly struck with the similarity of most of them and those I myself experienced. Further observation and enquiry led me to form the opinion that they were common to cases of drowning.

A singular circumstance, and one, perhaps, the reader may have observed himself, or have heard of before, is, that persons dying slowly, often imagine in a morning, and sometimes also during the day, that they have been comfortably reposing on the *green* sward; or that their bed is there, or in the open air, and that they are going farther away.

Dr. Winslow mentions the case of a man who was hanged, but, owing to the arrival of a reprieve, was cut down and resuscitated. Upon being asked "what his sensations were whilst hanging?" He replied, that "the preparations for his execution were dreadful and horrible beyond all expression, but that upon being 'dropped' he instantly found himself amid fields and rivers of blood, which gradually acquired a *greenish* tinge. Imagining that if he could reach a certain spot he would be easy, he seemed to himself to struggle forcibly to attain it, and then consciousness and all feeling were suspended." ("*Diseases of the Brain and Mind.*")

A well-known writer says, "Nothing can be concluded from struggles, shrinkings, and cries. A decapitated man, in whom all consciousness is necessarily entirely (?) obliterated, struggles to free his hands,

different ways, of which few, if any, are really satisfactory. The psychical nature of dreaming, as of sleep, will probably continue for ever inexplicable. The impossibility of accurately observing its phenomena throws insurmountable difficulties in the way of the investigator. It is, however, in the study of these phenomena that we can alone look for information, and from them alone can we hope to form rational opinions on the subject, since they are all that is within our reach.

The accession and character of dreams seem chiefly to depend on the suggestion of immediate influences, particularly external ones. Light, sounds, touch, any thing that can reach the mind through a partly sleeping sense, is sufficient for the purpose. Then the faculties which are more or less awake appear to 'run riot' on the imperfectly received or misinterpreted impression, and imagination unchecked by the other faculties, by reason and objective sense, continue the work. Memory lends her aid; one idea

attempts to stand upright, and stamps with his feet. A headless fly, fish, or worm, writhes and twists about if touched, although entirely (?) deprived of sensation. A fly makes the movement of brushing its eyes by reflex action, although its head may be off. Animals that fight with the hind legs use them vigorously, when decapitated, at every irritation applied to the nerves." (G. H. Lewes.) I cannot wholly agree with the conclusions drawn by this writer, although I admit the facts. I have myself seen a trunkless head loll out the tongue, and roll it from side to side, move the jaws and eyes, &c., twenty minutes after decapitation. The fact that a vigorous fowl, suddenly and cleanly decapitated, will, if set upon its legs, often run several feet, and even several yards, has probably been noticed by some of my readers.

Dr. Ernest Sansom observes, "Signs which are taken as evidences of pain are, I believe, frequently automatic expressions not actually indicative of suffering. We know that signs of pain are, under other circumstances, sometimes shown when none are felt. The shriek of pain is imitated by one who sees another in danger." With this I fully agree.

recalls another often unconnected with it, as in our waking hours; and the habits, disposition, and usual desires of the dreamer, commonly give a tone to the whole. As the poet says:—

"The potent will, by manly mind,
"Not even in sleep is quite resigned."

The thoughts floating in the mind as we fall asleep also appear to be a common source of dreams. The subject is rambled over loosely and irregularly for a time, and then suggests others; and thus a train of dreaming often continues until sleep becomes sufficiently deep to arrest it. It often happens that we are more or less awake during the hours we afterwards think we were asleep, when the thoughts that arise in the mind are continued, or become suggestive of others, giving rise to dreams, in the manner just mentioned.

In the above way the immediate cause and character of many dreams may be satisfactorily accounted for. Were it possible for us to know every thing that falls on the partly-sleeping senses, the subject that engaged the mind just before falling asleep, and the thoughts that arose during the short periods of being partially awake, no doubt the number might be very greatly extended, and, perhaps, so far as to include nearly all dreams, if not all of them.

I believe it is generally admitted that, in perfectly sound sleep we do not dream. Experience and observation also lead us to the conclusion that, in general, the degree of vividness forms a leading distinction between the images and sensations of the waking and the sleeping state. Remembered sensations and images are also usually fainter than actual ones; and thus dreams borrowed chiefly from the stores of memory, are fainter than those that arise from the immediate suggestions of the senses. In certain diseases, and under other occasional circumstances, the reverse of each of the preceding is, however, the case, and the visionary is more vivid than realities, and more impressed with ideas. It is also worthy of remark that abstract ideas commonly borrow from customary shapes, and that remembered forms maintain their entirety after they are known to have changed them, or to have ceased to exist. It is thus that ghosts appear in drapery;[1] and that scenes are reproduced in dreams, in all their details, although the party, when awake, knows that many of them have been removed, or have passed away.

Somnambulism[2] appears to be a form of dreaming in which nearly all the muscles are awake and active; and *Somniloquism*,[3] another form in which the voluntary muscles on which speech depends, are not only awake, but act more or less imperfectly in correspondence with the thoughts. A similar state to the last exists in persons who are in the habit of expressing their thoughts aloud, or 'talking to themselves,' without knowing it.

Delirium,[4] or the symptomatic wandering of the mind in fevers and certain inflammatory and brain diseases, when of an active or marked character, probably partakes of the nature of each of the three states last mentioned, the patient

---

[1] This fact, I think, clearly shows the absurdity of the belief in apparitions. If they were not purely imaginary, mere creations of a weak or disordered mind, or ocular deceptions, we may reasonably conclude that they would appear either naked, or in their shrouds, and not in articles of dress that are actually elsewhere, or, in many cases, long before worn out or destroyed.

[2] The act or practice of walking in one's sleep; from the L. *somnus* sleep, and *ambulo* I walk.

[3] Talking in one's sleep; from the L. *somnus*, and *loquor* I talk or speak.

[4] From the L. *deliro* I wander in mind, rave, or talk or think incoherently.

being apparently awake, but in reality only partially so. In its exaggerated forms it also approaches acute mania of a temporary or periodic kind. The quiet delirium of erysipelas—that variety which has chiefly to do with my narrative—is more closely related to dreaming than the others. Indeed, whether occurring by night, or by day, it closely resembles a continued day-dream of a varied and very vivid character occurring with the senses, or some of them, more awake than in what is popularly termed 'day-dreaming'; by which the sequence of ideas and illusions, though irregular, are usually more connected, persistent, and continuous, than in ordinary dreams. In general, as in dreaming, the illusions and irregular trains of thought primarily depend on the suggestions of immediate influences. Among these, sounds heard and misunderstood by the patient are the most prolific. His pains and sensations also act in the same way. The subject, the thoughts floating through his mind as he passes into a delirious state, likewise frequently furnish the groundwork on which his subsequent wanderings are raised. Then imagination begins her work, and memory supplies her stores to continue and diversify the vision or illusion. And lastly, the usual habits or bias of the mind in health, give a tone to the whole, and leave the thoughts rambling on a train of favourite subjects until the patient is aroused, or until he sinks into a state of actual sleep or stupor from exhaustion.

During delirium the whole character and disposition is developed. In its more violent forms, as it is in mania and drunkenness, all restraint of language and behaviour disappears, and the patient usually indulges in both to the full extent of his accustomed way, or that his disposition may lead him when in health.[1]

[1] Reflections on the preceding subjects often occupied me during my delirium. Some of them are combined in the above passing remarks.

In my own case there was hardly a subject or illusion that occupied my mind for any length of time, and which was of sufficient interest and intensity to be remembered, that I could not afterwards assign a cause for its accession and subsequent character. The suggestions of immediate influences, life-bias and habits, and a memory during health of an extraordinarily retentive character, which, even when disorganised by disease, kept throwing out disconnected fragments on the troubled waters of my mind, satisfactorily account for the whole. Feeling deeply interested in the subject, as soon as I was well enough to observe and make enquiries to elucidate it, I did so; and the results of my investigations support the statement I have just made.

In previous chapters I have given some examples of the operations of my mind, and the illusions which occupied it, at this period, and which will serve to illustrate the subjects to which] the above desultory remarks refer. They form, however, only a few, a very few of the subjects on which I maundered, and only a small, very small part of my wanderings. The relation of all those which I distinctly remember, even now, would fill several volumes. In my delirium time and space seemed to be annihilated, just as often occurs in ordinary dreaming; for the events of days, weeks, and even months, appeared to follow, in regular sequence, within a space of time that could not, even if they had occupied the whole of the night without interruption, have exceeded a few hours; and distant scenes very wide apart were visited in rapid succession during the same short period. A strange fact connected with these illusions, and with the whole time that I was continually in a delirious state, is, that with scarcely an exception, nothing appeared to be illuminated with full daylight. The nearest approach to it was usually light of that peculiar description that fell upon every thing. during the annular eclipse of the sun that I witnessed a few years since. More generally the light resembled twilight, or that of the dawn; but in all the happiest scenes in which I luxuriated, subdued violet-light prevailed, and tinted every object with a glow of magic beauty. This probably depended on the injuries my head had received, and the fevered state of my brain; and more immediately from my eyes being insensible to light, or only so in such a slight degree as to convey this impression to the optic nerve.[1]

Want of space prevents my giving the details of even a few of the other illusions that passed through my mind at this period. Three or four of the most remarkable of them, or which I should rather say, most interested me at the time, are briefly noticed below :—

At this period my attention was frequently occupied with imaginary operas, which I mentally both saw and heard with all the truthfulness of reality. They, however, differed from those of our opera-houses, in the plot, characters, scenery, and music, appearing real or natural, instead of operatic or theatrical. They all appeared to occur on the very scene on which the plot was laid; and the actors seemed to be the real parties, and not professional dramatis personæ. Among others, was one that I fancied I saw and heard several times, and which passed with me—why I cannot tell—as the "*Cotters of the Rhine.*" The plot though extremely simple was highly interesting to me; and the scenery and music, absolutely beautiful. No mere

---

[1] Another strange circumstance, not alluded to in the Text, was observed by me. There appeared to be a double action in my mind, and often rational thoughts were coincident with incoherent ones. Then there would appear to be a struggle, as of two principles, between them. Sometimes one of two trains of coexistent thought would outstrip the other. I must confess that this has strengthened my previous impression of the duality of the mind.

description of them can do them justice. The plot was laid on the banks of the Rhine, where I fancied I then was. The hero was the youngest son of a proud baron of ancient lineage, and had been cast forth from the paternal castle for the dire offence of having married, against the wishes of his sire, the heroine of the piece, the amiable and beautiful, but almost portionless daughter of an eminent sculptor living in a neighbouring town. The visions of happiness that formed their day-dreams before their union, were realised in their future life. They retired to a small cottage delightfully situated on the banks of the Rhine, and, amid some of the most beautiful scenery on that river, for a while forgot the world, forgot all but themselves and heaven. Their wants were few, and their mode of life inexpensive. For a time the personal effects which Henrich had brought with him from the castle, and the trifling dowry which Inez had received from her father, sufficed to meet all their wants. Gradually these scanty resources began to fail them. 'Poverty came in at the door,' but love did not 'fly out of the window.' On the contrary the latter rather increased than diminished; and the mutual sacrifices which they had to make under the circumstances only served the more to endear them to each other. Time passed on, and then the voices of two miniature reproductions of themselves were heard within the cottage. A couple of sweet children had blessed their union. The scenes in the garden, and at the cottage-door, just after the sun had sunk beneath the western horizon, were delightful in the extreme—Inez sitting beneath the trelliced porch partly screened by luxuriant climbing plants and flowers, with her harp accompanying the duetto, and Henrich gazing in tenderness first on her, and then on the little ones amusing themselves on the grass near their feet—who can describe it? Yet both the scene and the music was witnessed and heard by me. But now necessity, that 'fruitful mother of invention,' compelled Henrich to frequently turn his thoughts on more mercenary and worldly subjects. Soon he had elaborated a scheme, and proceeded to carry it out. He had a noble tenor voice which by training was perfectly under his control, and he was a composer of more than ordinary ability. Inez too was an accomplished singer, and an artist of no mean skill. He would compose a few operettas and some shorter pieces of music, which, with the works he already knew of other composers, would form a répertoire sufficient to start an itinerant operatic company which he would organise and conduct, and form a part of. Inez should be their prima donna; he their chief tenor. By sacrificing the remaining articles of jewelry and other valuables which they possessed, funds were raised just sufficient to carry out the undertaking in a very humble way. The scenery was painted by himself and Inez; a marquée of extraordinary proportions was hired, the necessary assistants engaged, and the experiment commenced. I was present at their first rehearsal—present at their début in their new characters. It occurred shortly before sunrise (!). Now came the continued persecution and interruption of the Baron, and the malevolent brothers, who did all they could to thwart the efforts of Henrich, to bring the enterprise to ruin, and to destroy the material connected with it. The plots and attempts against it, and the hair-breadth escapes, were numerous and exciting; but still the undertaking paid sufficiently to enable its projector and proprietor to live and to support in comfort his adored Inez, and his beloved children. At last the director of the royal opera-house of * * *, one of the great German capitals, happened to be in the village of * * *, at the time of Henrich's visit to it. By chance he strolled past the marquée. It attracted his notice, he paid his money at the door, and entered it, for the purpose, as he afterwards confessed, of 'having a laugh' at the affair. His attention was soon arrested by singers who, though supported by a meagre and inferior orchestre, acquitted themselves to admiration. He listened, admired, and at last became astonished at the originality and finished rendering of the music. As soon as the piece was over he sought the manager, learned the particulars from him, and ——. The nature of the interview may be inferred from what followed.

The performance just referred to, was the last one of the company with Henrich as its manager and proprietor. A few days afterwards he sold his operatic material and the good-will of the concern to another, and, with his family, left the neighbourhood. Within a month from this time the musical circles of the city of * * * were electrified by the sudden appearance of a new tenor and a new prima donna at the royal opera-house, of such rare powers that their praises were on every tongue, and the newspapers, for a time, engrossed almost wholly with them. The one was the despised and cast-off son of Baron * * * *; the other, the amiable and lovely daughter of the poor and aged sculptor, Herr * * *.

A few years later, Henrich and Inez retired into private life. He again repaired to the banks of his favourite river; and there, on the spot on which stood the cottage in which he had spent his early happy days with Inez, he built a chateau. In this, with his family and father-in-law, he passed the remainder of his life. Henceforth he was only heard of as Henrich * * *, the great composer, whose musical works were continually performed in all the opera-houses and concert-rooms of both the old and the new world. His company was sought after by the great and noble; and even monarchs visited him in his retirement, and invited him and Inez to their courts. His last musical piece, and his chef-d'œuvre, was his requiem performed at the funeral of the aged sculptor, Herr * * *.

The concluding scene of the opera just referred to—the sweetest one that occurred in it—was a reproduction of Henrich and Inez sitting, just after sunset, on the same lawn on which I had seen them years before when inhabitants of the humble cottage, now changed into a magnificent chateau, with a youthful Henrich, and a second Inez even more beautiful than her mother, seated beside them, all in happiness and health together.[1]

Then a balloon-excursion round the world occupied much of my attention, and greatly interested me. It was full of incidents and adventures of a very exciting character. The balloon, and the machinery connected with it, were designed entirely by myself; and the whole scheme, and the method by which it was carried out, were extremely novel. Its construction occupied me daily for more than three months. The leading points of novelty about it were, that it was inflated with pure hydrogen-gas produced by voltaic batteries carried in it, so as to be available to supply the loss of gas that necessarily occurred on the journey. The quantity of gas used for inflation was only sufficient to raise the balloon and its appendages to a height of five or six hundred feet,

[1] The origin of this opera in my mind (and so of others) was, undoubtedly, my obscurely hearing a patient in a neighbouring bed singing German airs, mostly of a plaintive character, and one of them particularly so. This gentleman, a German, was lying there with a broken leg, and in the evening and early night was continually ' humming ' airs of his ' fatherland ' to while away the time. Whenever I heard them my mental wanderings took a musical and very genial tone.

by which communication with the surface of the earth passed over might be established at will, and easy stages taken, as circumstances might dictate. To raise the machine to higher altitudes gravitation-pumps were attached to it, by working which its attraction to the earth's centre might be so reduced, or in other words, its weight might be so lessened, that any elevation, within the limits of respirable atmosphere, might be easily attained. I had found, by long observation, that the winds that blow at the surface of the earth do not extend far upwards, and that at an elevation of a few miles there is a constant current of the air from each pole toward the tropics; that immediately above this current there is a deep stratum of quiescent air; and then a current of warm air running from the tropics to the poles, in a contrary direction to the first one. That, still higher, there is a perpetual current of air round the earth from east to west, or contrary to its diurnal motion, and which extends to the utmost limits of the atmosphere. A knowledge of these assumed facts enabled us, by ascending or descending, as circumstances indicated, to direct our course in any way we chose; and to communicate with the earth, or even to alight on it, when we thought proper. In this way we were entirely masters of our course and position, and could conduct the voyage in any manner we pleased. Our first attempt at starting proved a failure; but after making certain improvements in the machine suggested by experience, we made a successful ascent from Chiswick Ait, one fine morning, just before sunrise. The trip occupied a month, during which we made several important geographical and meteorological discoveries, which I cannot now stay to relate. Among the trophies we brought back with us were a fine young lion which we hooked up with our grappling-irons in crossing over Africa, and a Patagonian and an Esquimaux obtained in the same manner.

Next came a very interesting voyage in the steam-yacht *Daphne*, during which we discovered the north-west passage and the long-conjectured inner polar-sea, with a host of incidents and wonders which may easily be imagined to occur or exist in those regions.

A second voyage of the steam-yacht Daphne led to the discovery of the antarctic continent, and the inner antarctic sea with its wondrous archipelago, and its curious inhabitants. We had been skirting along the edge of the ice for about three weeks, when we found it bend southward, forming, as we thought, an enormous bay. We kept the head of the yacht toward the south for several days, until we found ourselves in a current running due south at the rate of several 'knots' per hour. By the next day this current had so increased in rapidity and violence that we lost our 'dead-reckoning;' and, the weather being very cloudy, we could not see the heavenly bodies. We were thus unable accurately to determine our position, or the rate at which we moved. We, however, concluded that we were in a great gulf that communicated with some inner sea. Our coals and provisions, on examination, being found only sufficient to last us another month, it was not deemed prudent to go farther in the same direction at present. It was determined among us that we should proceed to the nearest port, and then, after 're-coaling' and 're-victualing' the yacht, return and explore the opening in the ice which we had so happily discovered. The yacht was therefore put about, and, with her head direct north, we put on all our steam for the purpose of retracing our course as quickly as possible. The effort was, however, soon found useless, owing to the current running faster south than the rate of the yacht north, by which she fell astern at the rate of five or six 'knots' an hour. What was to be done? After a general council held on the quarter-deck, it was determined to let the yacht go with the current, to keep our fires 'banked-up,' and to husband our coal for any future emergency. The yacht was then again put about, and a fore-topsail set, just to give her steerage way. We continued our course southward for some days. The temperature of the air on leaving the bay was cold in the extreme, and the wind piercing. It had gradually suffered an agreeable change, and was now comfortably warm. This raised our hopes, and great expectations were entertained by all of us that we should make some discoveries on this voyage even more wonderful than those in the preceding one. At length the fog that had surrounded us for several days cleared off, and we 'sighted' land on our starboard bow. As we neared it, we could perceive through our glasses that it was covered with herbage and trees, and presented the general appearance of land in the northern portions of the temperate zone. We kept the land in sight for another twenty-four hours, and then emerged into the open sea which lay beyond and south of it. We now found the current which had borne us forward rapidly failing us, and so we again 'got up' our steam to bear us on our course. The temperature of the air was now as mild and agreeable as that of a May-day in England, and the wind merely sufficient to gently ruffle the sea around us. The experienced eye of the captain soon led him to form the opinion that we might expect to 'sight' land ahead of us before long. In another hour "land ahead" was shouted by the look-out in the fore-top. All of us were at once on the qui vive; and soon we could dimly perceive land before us through our glasses from the deck. In another hour we were within two or three miles of it. We 'coasted' it for some time, gradually and cautiously approaching it. We could now perceive that it possessed remarkable fertility, and was inhabited. We could even see some of the natives on the shore, and could detect dwellings and villages at no great distance from it. We also concluded, from our observations of the coast, that it was an island. By-and-by we found a suitable inlet in which we determined to effect a landing. The vessel was therefore brought to an anchor, and a boat lowered and manned. Besides being provided with a variety of presents for the natives, the boat's crew, of which I was one, carried side-arms and revolvers; a precaution which, as the reader will presently see, was quite unnecessary.

On landing we were met by some of the natives, who endeavoured, by signs, to impress on us that we were quite safe among them, and then invited us to a neighbouring town or village. Their dress and general appearance, and manners, particularly attracted our notice, as ours apparently did theirs. They were of an oriental character which carried the mind back to the patriarchal ages, and closely resembled what is still seen in Palestine or the Holy Land. On reaching the village we were introduced to some persons who appeared to be the elders or principal men of the place, from whom we received the most marked kindness and attention. A repast, of which we all partook, followed. It was remarkable only on account of the absence of the flesh of animals or meat, though fish was there. They next tried to amuse us in various ways by shewing us objects of interest, and after inviting us, by signs, to repeat our visit, conducted us to the spot on the shore at which our boat lay.

We returned to the ship highly gratified with our visit, and with the treatment we had received from the natives. Shortly afterwards, at a general council, we determined to remain where we were until we had acquainted ourselves with the new country and people we had so luckily discovered. The chief difficulty in the way of our obtaining information respecting either of them, lay in our entire ignorance of their language; but this we trusted to get over after a time. The next day we again landed, and this second visit proved still more satisfactory to us than the first one. Among other incidents that occurred during it was one that, though apparently trifling, led to very important results. On my taking a piece of folded paper from my waistcoat pocket to make some memorandum, their attention was attracted towards it; and they appeared greatly interested in the writing when I shewed it to them. One of them handed me some of their writing, on which I perceived that it closely resembled the Coptic, if it were not actually in that ancient language; and on my reading some words from it they appeared greatly surprised and pleased. I therefore determined to devote all my energies to acquire their language, as the readiest means of obtaining a knowledge of them and their country. By adopting the method taught me by Mezzofanti, I made very rapid progress. In about a fortnight I was able to make them understand what I referred to when I asked them for any thing I wanted. Within a month I could converse with them, though imperfectly, on all common subjects; and within three months, was quite familiar with their language. During this period we visited many of the other islands, and by short trips in the yacht, for two or three days at a time, under the guidance of a native pilot, and with myself for an interpreter, we were able to 'lay down' a rough chart or map of a large portion of the sea and islands around us, and to acquire much information from the natives. In this way I learned the following particulars respecting them :—

The part I was now in, or which I should rather say, I made my 'head quarters,' was an island, of some thirty or forty miles in circumference, forming a portion of a vast archipelago situated in the inner antarctic sea, and extending to within four or five degrees of the south pole. The climate was delightful, and reminded me of that of the table-land of Quito. Eternal spring seemed to reign there; and its animal and vegetable productions were of a corresponding character. The warmth and genial nature of the climate arose, as I afterwards discovered, from the heated air of the tropics which, ascending into the higher regions of the atmosphere, flows toward the pole and then descends and flows over the surface of the part, by some peculiar species of attraction, the nature of which I could not ascertain. The surface of this current high above them and before it reaches them, furnishes them with light resembling subdued sunlight. There is thus no true night there; but the diurnal period of twenty-four hours is divided into two portions of activity and repose, corresponding to the day and night of the temperate zones.

The way the part became populated appeared to me extremely singular. I learned that Rameses the Great, who flourished some thirteen or fourteen centuries before our era, adopted the plan of sending out shiploads of colonists to form settlements, or factories as they have been called in later times, on certain points of the coasts of distant nations his people traded with, in order to extend and protect the commerce of his empire. A squadron of this kind being dispersed during a tempest, one of the ships composing it, after losing all traces of their proper course, and beating about on the ocean for many weeks, was drawn here by powers beyond their control, in the same way as the yacht Daphne, with ourselves, had been. From the people of this ship, whose number, after their losses at sea, did not exceed fifty souls, had sprung the whole population of the archipelago, now amounting, as I was told, to nearly three millions.

The present language is a dialect of the ancient Coptic which gradually arose out of the parent language, and does not differ from it more than the present English does from that of the time of Chaucer and his cotemporaries.

The simplicity and purity of the life and manners of this strange people greatly surprised and pleased me. Vice, poverty, misery, and war, are unknown among them; whilst pride, drunkenness, dishonesty, and falsehood, are so rare, that one of their elders assured me he could remember only one or two instances of them during his long life. The government is purely patriarchal, if government it may be called, of which the only duties consist in being occasionally called upon to arbitrate on doubtful or disputed questions or rights. Gaols and workhouses, and even policemen, do not exist there. Courts of law and justice there are none; since there are no legal disputes to settle, and no criminals to try and punish. Corporal punishment is never resorted to by them, even for children. Gunpowder and weapons of offence are also unknown to them. They never shed blood, not even that of animals for the table. Ordinary animal-food forms no part of their diet, which consists chiefly of fish, eggs, edible birdsnests, and grain, fruit, and other vegetables. Their chief beverages are water and a kind of weak wine formed of the fermented juices of mixed fruits common to the part. They are unacquainted with alcohol, and with the art of distillation in any form. Wood and sea weed form their only fuel. Their domestic animals are of few species; but very prolific. They are all of an oriental character, having sprung from those which the ancestors of this people brought with them from Egypt. Among them I noticed the horse, a beautiful variety of the ass of remarkable sagacity and docility and much prized, and two or three varieties of the dog. The kind way in which they are universally treated offers an instructive lesson to the inhabitants of our own and other countries that pride themselves on their Christianity and civilization. There is no recourse to the lash, stick, kicking, or other sources of torture, to break them in, or to command obedience; or, as we often see in our streets, to indicate to the poor animal what he is expected to do. Owing to the regularity of the lives and habits of this people, the simple nature of their diet, and their ignorance of the use of spirituous liquors, they are seldom afflicted with disease, and attain to an extreme old age without exhibiting any material symptoms of decay; and when death comes, it usually resembles a mere falling asleep to wake no more. Hence it is that there are no hospitals among them, and no professional surgeons; but some of the elders study medicine and surgery, and attend their neighbours gratuitously when their services are required, which is seldom. In the few cases of sickness which occur, the neighbours of the afflicted parties vie with each other in attending them, and in supplying the wants of the sufferers. Sometimes, though rarely, it happens that in certain islands of the archipelago the harvest fails, or is scanty, in some particular article of food or necessary of life; in which cases an ample supply is immediately sent them voluntarily from the other islands, not in the way of trade, but as presents. Science and literature has made little progress among them. The latter consists chiefly of bardic lore, collected traditions, songs, histories, and moral tales, with a few simple works that were brought with them from the land their ancestors emigrated from. All, however, that is necessary to the well-being and happiness of man, and to the rational enjoyment of life, is known to them, or abounds among them.

After spending some four months in exploring the islands within our reach, and obtaining all the information we could from their inhabitants, we bethought ourselves of returning home. How to effect this was a question that puzzled us. We had ascertained that the only communication between the inner sea and the ocean was the gulf by which we entered it, and that the violence and direction of its current never varied. The yacht was, therefore, useless to us beyond the limits of the sea we were now in. After much consultation and debate, we determined to construct two balloons of sufficient size to carry our party, and then to await a favourable wind to bear us northward, when we hoped to reach some island or continent where we could meet with a ship or vessel that would convey us home. In constructing these balloons the natives afforded us all the assistance in their power, although they did not appear to clearly understand the nature of the attempt we were about to make. When we told them we must leave them, they exhibited considerable emotion and regret, and endeavoured to persuade us either to remain permanently with them, or to delay our departure for a time.

The balloons having been constructed, we kept them constantly in readiness for use, so as to be able to avail ourselves of the first favourable wind. We next presented the yacht Daphne to the chief patriarch of the archipelago, and seizing our opportunity, took our departure from the people we had so strangely discovered. As we ascended from among them, some few waved their adieus; but the larger number gazed after us as if they were lost in admiration and wonder.

After a few hours the direction of the two balloons slightly varied, by which they parted company. The one I was in, after a successful, but very cold passage of three days, descended on the coast of South America, near Monte Video. Here we were so fortunate as to meet with a homeward-bound ship about to sail the next day, in which our party obtained a passage. In this way we arrived safely home, exactly fifteen months after leaving it. The other balloon and its passengers had not been heard of six months after my arrival home, which was the apparent time at which my vision closed.[1]

The search for ancient MSS. of an antiquity greater than any at present known to exist, frequently occupied my mind at this period, as may be inferred from a previous chapter. An impression seemed to have taken possession of me, that some of those of the antediluvian and earlier post-diluvial ages were still existing, and were discoverable by patient and untiring search. The desire also haunted me to construct a universal alphabet and language, of such a simple and inviting kind, that it would be immediately adopted by all nations, however dissimilar their present languages may be.

Another series of frequently recurring adventures in which I appeared to be engaged, occurred in 'patent extemporaneous houses,' which, with their fittings, were formed of peculiarly constructed mattresses, which could be put together and taken apart, and removed from place to place, with great facility, and of which the lightness and inexpensiveness I fancied were no slight advantages.

---

[1] The origin of this, as well as of the two immediately preceding visions, I assign to the suggestive influence of certain patients near me reading aloud some book of voyages and discoveries, and conversing on the subject; which I must have heard imperfectly, and misinterpreted.

Then almost nightly (it must have been early morning) came 'shifting of beds,' for which purpose I appeared to resort to every possible expedient. My own bed was torture to me—long lying in it on my back had rendered it absolutely intolerable. I was constantly endeavouring to change my position and place in it, but could do so only to the extent of an inch or two. Then I fancied I had succeeded (how I could not tell) in reaching another bed newly made, that was softer. O, how comfortable it felt for a short time! Then to another, and another, until the end of a ward, which seemed to me to be several hundred yards in length, was reached. Next—how pleasant! I had passed the open doors, and was lying in one of the beds placed outside them in the open air. The breeze felt so cool and refreshing, it was delightful! Then came the usual fit of drowsiness characteristic of a delirious, restless night, and the dread that I should be unable to get back to my own bed before I fell asleep, and that the 'sister' would come and chide me for being absent from it. Finally, heavy sleep or stupor closed the scene.

*   *   *   *   *

Such were some of the vagaries which distempered thought and fancy played me in the hours of my delirium. To continue their relation further would be repetition ad absurdum; and, perhaps, some of my readers might add, ad nauseum; as a certain sameness, or tone, always pervades the wanderings of the same mind.

Before closing this chapter I may add that all, or nearly all my delirium, was of a more or less pleasant kind, and entirely confined to subjects, scenes, pursuits, and adventures, which no thoughtful or well-regulated mind need blush to own. My wanderings, as a rule, were also confined to myself; and were not, as is commonly the case in most other diseases, a source of annoyance to my fellow-patients.[1]

[1] I only recollect, and from enquiries I have made can only learn of, *one* instance where it was otherwise. One night there had been a little noisy joking going on, between two or three of the patients and one of the nurses, which ended, I believe, in some little altercation between two of the latter. I misunderstood what was occurring, and thought that they were abusing and ill-using poor M——. Being suddenly alarmed, I struggled to raise myself in bed, and called out incoherently about it. My nurse was instantly by my side to explain the matter, and in a few minutes I was pacified.

CHAPTER XI.

Personal state and progress—crisis—subsequent debility—treatment, diet, medicines—attendants—improvement—first sense of light—daily routine—misadventure—bandages v. splints—tumefaction of head—operation—prospects—unfortunate incident, hæmorrhage—generous diet—further improvement—something to laugh at—hysterical attacks — recollections—the heart's misgivings — recovered sight, reading—learning to walk—employment of time —visitors—presents—flowers—that head again—cold-water pads, poultices—thoughts of home—progress—short relapse—scrubbing-brush Philippics—amusing incidents—approaching departure, &c.

AT length the crisis was passed, but not the danger. The recession of the disease was slow, remarkably slow; and for days I remained in a state in which death appeared not merely likely, but imminent. The symptoms of exhaustion and debility were so extreme that, apart from others, it appeared very probable that I should sink under them. The efforts of my medical attendants were, therefore, now chiefly directed to the administration of stimulants, and nourishment in a condensed and easily assimilable form, to sustain me under them, and to enable me to rally. The state of my head and face was particularly alarming. They were still horribly distended and of a fiery aspect, and the discharge from them continually oozed through the pores of the skin, often running down like water from a sponge. It was many days before this sensibly began to lessen; and even then the discharge continued for a considerable time afterwards. The delirium also continued, and only gradually abated with the more urgent symptoms of the disease. The wounds in my throat and the side of my head had shared the usual fate in such cases, and had become greatly aggravated in severity. They were now, with the neighbouring parts, in an extremely swollen, inflamed, and painful state, and poured out a continual discharge of pus which was most annoying; and this continued with little abatement for weeks. The right side of my head too, extending to the back and upper part, days after the erysipelatous swelling had partially subsided, began to suppurate; and soon a large collection of pus was formed between the scalp and the plates of the skull, separating them, and forming a tumour of an alarming character. At first it appeared doubtful whether this tumefaction was due to an accumulation of the ordinary erysipelatous discharge (serum), or to pus or matter; but in a few days its real character became unmistakable. It did not gradually lessen in quantity, as the former usually does by oozing through the pores of the skin; but remained permanent, and its quantity and the distension of the part increased daily. Ultimately a surgical operation was found necessary for its removal, to which I shall allude hereafter. I was still unable to see. Every thing appeared involved in mist and gloom. Even objects held close to me, and persons leaning over me, appeared like shadowy forms or profiles floating in the semi-darkness.

My diet at this time consisted of beef-tea and eggs beaten up with wine or brandy, which were ordered on my bed-ticket, in the manner noticed in a previous chapter. I was to lack nothing of the kind I could take; and every thing thus ordered was supplied, of the best quality, by the hospital. The strong expression of opinion by certain competent and experienced persons that, the only way to save me was to support me with abundance of nourishment and stimulants, led my wife to urgently request the chief house-surgeon to permit her to increase my allowance of the latter, which she offered to provide herself. He kindly assured her, that he had ordered the largest quantity which he thought would be safe or desirable in my case; and that had more been needed, it should have been provided by the hospital, to any extent required, regardless of the expense; and that the same would be done for the future. My allowance of eggs was, I think, four or five per day. This number M—— thought she might safely increase; and hence brought with her daily some six or seven more of the finest kind she could procure, and placed them with the others in my drawer. One of these eggs she beat up about every hour, and administered to me either with a spoon or the baby's feeding-cup. Fortunately my stomach never failed me, but digested every thing I took. To this I owe my ultimate recovery. Had it been otherwise I must have sunk under the frightful exhaustion and debility produced by my wounds and the disease.

My medicines at this time were entirely of a stimulant and tonic character—bark, quinine, ammonia, saffron, with opium or morphia occasionally, according to the symptoms.

I think it was a few days after I had passed the crisis, that I missed Mr. D——, the kind and attentive surgeon who had first attended me; and who had been so assiduous in his attentions to me up to this point. On enquiry, I found his term of office had expired, and that he had left the hospital. He was one of those men whose affable manners, amiable disposition, and goodness of heart, were only equalled by his surgical skill and habitual attention to his patients. His tenderness and delicacy in whatever examination or operation he was engaged, no less endeared him to all, than the kind and soothing tones of his voice awakened their hope and confidence. As I afterwards learned, he was a general favourite in the ward, where his presence inspired every one with joy and new life; and his attendance was the highest boon the patients sought to obtain. My prayers for his welfare followed him.

The gentleman who now took my case almost entirely under his care, was Mr. T——, the chief house-surgeon, of whom I have before spoken. I found him also to be a most kind and gentlemanly man, and most assiduous in his attentions to me. He regularly visited and examined me every morning, during his usual round of the wards; and, for weeks, not a single night passed that he did not come to my bedside and enquire how I was, and see if any thing more could be done for me. He also, for some time, during the worst part of my case, usually came to see me at least once else during the day. He likewise very kindly told me that, at any hour of the day or night I might conceive his presence necessary, he would immediately come to me on my sending the nurse for him. What more could he do or say? His deputy, Mr. M——, the assistant house-surgeon who replaced Mr. D——, was also very kind and attentive to me. Indeed, all the surgical staff of the hospital were so; and, perhaps, it may appear scarcely fair to name one more than another, since they all did their best for me.

My nurse too, Mrs. P.,— a very experienced and clever woman in her way, who had served under Miss Nightingale in the hospitals of the Crimea—was also most kind and attentive to me at this period. Then there was Mrs. D——, the matron or good 'sister' of the ward, to whom I cannot accord too much praise. She superintended every thing, and did all she could, and all her great experience suggested, to cheer me up and save me. It was chiefly under her excellent advice that my wife acted. And the last! how could I ever fully repay her for her constant kindness and untiring attendance on me—her noble devotion, her self-sacrifice—from the beginning to the end of my afflictions. Alas! alas! I can now never repay the debt of gratitude I owe her.

With such care and attention as I have described, it would have been, as one of my fellow sufferers in the ward observed, "hard, indeed, if he does not get over it;" a remark with which the reader will probably agree. At least, I had every chance to do so, as far as human skill and assistance could avail. Happily Providence sustained me through my trials, and blessing the efforts made in my behalf, ultimately raised me from that bed of sickness which had been so nearly also one of death. "What, O Lord, can I render unto thee for all thy mercies?"

A change for the better, though a slight one, now gradually became perceptible, and hopes of my recovery began to be entertained. The immediate source of danger had passed away; but still it was doubtful, in the state I was in, whether I should not ultimately sink under the debility left by the united action of my accidents and the disease that had afflicted me. It was certain, that under the most favourable circumstances, my convalescence would be long and tedious. I was physically prostrated, so entirely prostrated, the vital energy so feeble, that I was as helpless as an infant, or even more so. And so I hung on, as it were, to life for some days longer, still improving, but so gradually, that the difference of a day or two was scarcely apparent. It was early on one of these mornings that I had, for the first time since my illness, a faint perception of light, a vision promising recovery, an illusion that made a great impression on me at the time, and which is still vividly remembered. Suddenly something appeared to rest upon me, and to surround me, which was perceptible to every sense. The sensation over the whole surface of my body resembled that produced by sunlight on the closed eyes. Then the vision described in Job flashed through my mind. "'A spirit passed before my face. It stood still, but I could not discern the form thereof. An image was before mine eyes, there was silence, and I heard a voice saying ' Shall mortal man be more just and merciful than God? Shall man be more pure than his maker? Behold they that dwell in houses of clay, whose foundation is in the dust, are crushed before the moth. They are destroyed from morning to evening; they perish for ever without any regarding it. Doth not their excellency pass away? They die, even without wisdom. Wilt thou perish like them, or live? God will try thee yet again. Live, and sin no more!'" Such was the interpretation of the passage in my mind.[1] I looked up, and had an obscure perception of light, which nevertheless seemed to me like rays of glory. As I raised my eyelids I fancied that a luminous form, like that pictured of the archangels, rose from the foot of my bed towards the ceiling, and instantly disappeared.[2] By a

[1] It will be seen that it varies slightly from the original, and that the last three sentences were of my own creation.

[2] I beg the reader will not assume from my relation of this vision, that I refer it to supernatural influence. On the contrary, I refer it to natural causes. I afterwards ascertained that the sun, which had not been seen for a long time, suddenly broke through the clouds that morning. It awakened me, and the comparative gloom that in a few minutes resulted from its being again obscured by clouds, produced the spectral illusion, which was purely ocular. It recalled to my disordered mind, at the moment of being suddenly aroused from sleep or inco-

strange coincidence, from this moment I began to slowly recover my sight; and though my perception of objects still continued obscure for a long time, and the air appeared misty and full of 'muscæ volitantes,'[1] yet I could see and distinguish them one from another, which was a great comfort to me. From this hour also I began to improve in a manner which, though still slow, was clearly perceptible day by day.

The daily routine of my surgical treatment, medicines, and diet, continued much the same as previously described —the same washings, dressings, cotton-wool, &c., as before; with, at intervals, renewal or tightening of the bandages that held my arm in its place, and my collar-bone together. In general Mr. T—— attended to these bandages, and the way he acquitted himself of the task, as well as his great personal experience, rendered me very anxious that he should always do so. On one occasion, however, Mr. M—— applied a new one. He conceived my right shoulder had sunk a little—I dare say it had—and he kindly endeavoured to remedy the evil by raising the shoulder, applying a pad under the upper part of the arm, and then very tightly bandaging the arm to my side, and my fore-arm and hand in their places, as before. The operation gave me great pain, though I did not complain of it; and after some hours this became so intolerable that I was compelled to get the nurse to remove the pad. By some unfortunate mishap, either at the time of applying the pad and bandages, or

herence, its favourite book of Job, and a fertile imagination did the rest. Still it made a deep and lasting impression on me. The coincidence of a fit of sunlight, a sudden improvement in my case, and the thoughts referred to, was nevertheless remarkable.

[1] Literally, 'flying flies'; the term applied by the faculty to the 'blacks,' &c., apparently seen floating in the air when the brain or eyes are disordered.

subsequent to it, the edges of the partly united fracture were torn asunder and misplaced; from which the reparation of the fracture was delayed, and a weak, irregular, and imperfect junction formed, that renders the arm and shoulder on that side extremely feeble.[1]

The tumefaction of my head still continued, and its condition at length demanded immediate relief. It had resisted all the usual methods of treatment—compression, cold-water pads, dressings, &c.—to promote absorption or dispersion. Mr. H. H——, on one of his rounds with the students of his class, devoted much attention to it, and delivered a short clinical lecture on it. I was raised up in bed on the occasion, and well remember what took place. After examining it himself, Mr. H—— pointed out to his pupils the respective distinctions between suppuration and collection of matter between the scalp and the skull and the ordinary humid puffiness of the scalp attending erysipelas, as well as the difference detectable by the fingers on manipulation. Then I felt a score or more of eager fingers tapping and manipulating the tumour in order that their owners might acquaint themselves practically with what had been

[1] I am much averse to the use of mere bandages for fractures of the collar-bone, as is now general in our hospitals, as well as in private practice. I never knew a *perfect* union made in this way, in a single difficult or complicated case. In simple cases, particularly in the young, when the patient is otherwise strong and healthy, they may do very well; but otherwise, the union is almost always defective and irregular. The use of the 'clavicular splint' is general in the French and German hospitals, even in the case of children. One formed of very stout, perforated pasteboard, on Dr. Foucart's plan, is the best that can be used, being both effective and comfortable to wear.

The day following my arrival in the hospital, and frequently afterwards, I requested that the bandages might be replaced by a splint; but was told that there were none in the hospital, and that it was not their practice to use them.

taught them by their professor. Mr. H—— concluded by observing that in such a well-defined case as the present one, all attempts to produce absorption or dispersion of the matter failed. The only remedy was bold incisions completely through the scalp with the knife; and that on his next visit this must be done, as further delay would be dangerous. On his next visit the examination, &c., of my head was repeated, and he directed that it should be opened at once; at the same time jocosely observing to Mr. T——, whom he charged with the operation, to "avoid the coronal artery." Mr. H. H——'s directions were carried out within an hour after his departure. The nurse being suddenly required to assist the operator, I held the basin against my throat to catch the blood and matter, although I had hardly strength to do so. The most painful part of the job was the tightly pinching up of the frightfully sensitive scalp by the operator before making the incisions; the pain resulting from the knife, though sharp, being trifling compared to it. However, I did not flinch from either of them. I think that about ¾ths of a pint of matter and black blood must have flowed into the basin from the wounds. The wounds were then dressed with an enormous poultice or cold-water dressing—I forget which it was now, but think it was the first, and my head then 'done up' in the usual way with cotton-wool and rollers. I was then laid back in bed; and must candidly confess that I felt relieved by the operation. The whole being over, I was complimented, by Mr. T——, on the way I had borne it. The truth was I saw the necessity of the operation, and was anxious it should be done. It would have been folly to have embarrassed the operator by any display of cowardice. There was, however, one near me looking on, whom it differently affected. My poor wife nearly fainted. It was too much for her. I shall have to allude to this unfortunate and obstinate head again; and will, therefore, now merely remark, that independent of the tumefaction and wounds, it continued still to emit erysipelatous matter for weeks, which poured forth and ran down over me every time I was raised up, or afterwards sat up, in bed. I was hence continually compelled not only to have my head surrounded with cotton-wool, but even to have huge rolls and wads of it on my cheeks and across my throat in order to absorb as much of the discharge as possible.

The same day that my head was opened my usual daily allowance of wine and brandy was replaced by eight ounces of gin, which was continued until I left the hospital. This was ordered as preferable to the former, from being less inflammatory, though sufficiently tonic and stimulating for my case. It was to be taken, in portions, with water, during the day. I always had an aversion to gin, and consequently, the next day, begged my chief surgeon to discontinue it, or to allow me to have one-half the quantity of brandy in its place; but he assured me it was necessary in my case, and that, without it, I should be less able to throw off the disease, and have less chance of recovery. I found it very pure, and of excellent quality; but still it was a long time before I relished it. It certainly did me much good; and on two different days in which my prejudice against such things led me to omit taking it, I found myself rapidly getting worse, and was glad to have recourse to it again.

The outer skin, particularly of my face and upper part of my body, had now been for some time coming off in flakes or scales like bran, leaving the surface beneath it exquisitively sensitive and tender. ' This continued for some time, and whilst it lasted the sense of irritation was occasionally so great, that I could scarcely restrain myself from tearing off my bandages to relieve it. The sensibility of the whole surface of my body had now become so extreme that it appeared to be slightly endued with the power of some of the other senses than 'touch.' I could perceive a person walking past or near my bed, even though at a distance of some yards, by the motion of the air it occasioned; whilst the undulations of sound fell on my skin, even through the bed-clothes, like little waves of air.

Another incident occurred about this time which threw me back considerably, and nearly cost me my life. It is, perhaps, worth relating, as showing the continual hazards that beset an accident-patient, even when he is progressing favourably. I had passed a day in more than usual comfort, and flattered myself that the wound which separated my ear from my face and ran down into my throat was improving, and would shortly heal. I lay hopeful and grateful, though restless and pained by the sameness of my long recumbent position, with my mind wandering, at intervals, on scenes far away, dozing and waking by turns, when one, or more, of the blood-vessels in the wound just mentioned, that had had their coats thinned by the suppurative action around them, gave way, and bled profusely. The blood streamed down my face and neck,[1] and over the upper part of my chest, saturating everything. I called out "Nurse! nurse!" but my feeble voice was unheard even by the patients in the two beds beside me, who always, when they heard me, repeated my calls. After several unsuccessful efforts to arouse attention I quietly resigned myself to my fate, well-knowing that I should either bleed to death, or

---

[1] Although I always lay upon my back I was compelled to turn my neck so as to keep the right side of my head upwards, as I could not bear the pillow to touch the injured side.

that the fainting that would be induced by the hæmorrhage would ultimately arrest it. Thus I lay. I felt the warm, vital stream gushing forth and running over me, but was unable to do more than mark its progress, and to moralise on the misfortune, until gradually increasing faintness rendered me unconscious. It must have been some time before twelve o'clock when this accident happened; and allowing an hour to have elapsed before I fainted, I must have lain in this state more than six hours before assistance reached me. The day-nurse—my own nurse, as I called her—was the first to discover it soon after she came on duty in the morning. The night-nurse excused herself on the occasion by saying, that on each of her visits to my bed she found me apparently sleeping so calmly, that she thought it would be wrong to disturb me.[1] On being aroused I was almost exsanguinous, with scarcely any life left in me. I was covered with blood. My shirt, flannel-shirt, the voluminous bandages about me, the pillows and sheets, were all soaked and stiffened with blood, and had to be changed for others. The washing I had to undergo, and the removal of bandages and linen, proved horribly distressing to me. I was afterwards told, that my eyes were sunken so deep in my head, and my features appeared so ghastly and lifeless, that I resembled a corpse rather than a living being; and the bed on which I lay, the floor of a slaughter-house. However, by the due administration of stimulants and nourishment, and by excessive care and attention, I rallied from this mishap after a time; but it threw my progress back some eight or ten days.

[1] Had she looked closely, one would think that she must have seen the blood on the pillow, &c. It is, however, only right to remark that, as only one gas-light is kept burning in the ward after nine at night, and that is turned down rather low, there is little light thrown on the patients' beds.

After the effects of the unfortunate event, just alluded to, had worn off, I began to progress a little faster. My appetite improved, and I was able to take a little solid food. I was now stinted in nothing. Every thing that I desired or could take, or which was suggested by others, was supplied me. Not an hour passed but what I had an egg beaten up, or some beef-tea, or new milk. My poor M—— was constantly by my side, ready with something to give me. Indeed, in her kindness, she almost 'bored' me with them. In addition to these things, I was supplied with the usual 'full diet' of the hospital, including an allowance of a pint of stout daily, besides my gin. Of this, of course, I could take but little at first; yet still I took a part of it, and the old saying is "every little helps." M—— used to sit by my side at dinner-time, and mince up some of the juiciest bits of roasted beef or mutton in the plate brought me, and with a little potato mashed with gravy, put it into my mouth. In this way I was able to take, perhaps, two or three ounces at a time. A little while afterwards, and I was further supplied with a plate of oysters daily for my lunch—beautiful natives they were, and I found them very relishing and refreshing. At the end of another fortnight or three weeks I was able to consume nearly the whole of every thing allowed me, but the bread, of which I could only get through a little. My breakfast now consisted of tea with eggs beaten up in it, and a finger, or two, of toast. My tea in the afternoon also generally consisted of the same. My appetite ultimately became so good, that I relished and digested every thing I took. Nothing that was suitable to an invalid came amiss or disagreed with me. My dinner was now supplemented with a nicely broiled mutton-chop, which, however, I did not eat at dinner. M—— used to put it into the drawer of my table or whatnot, and keep it back for my supper. And thus things went on, as to diet, until I left the building; and therefore the subject need not be again alluded to.

After reading the above description, the reader will probably observe to himself that, if any thing would restore my strength, and hasten my recovery, this treatment would do so. It happily did so to a very great extent; and I believe, as I have before remarked, that to it chiefly I owe being now able to write this narrative. The tonic and stimulating medicines which I took were chiefly useful in giving tone to the stomach and primæ viæ under this generous diet.

For some time I was every morning lifted out of bed by the nurse, and placed in a kind of arm-chair by its side, while she made the bed and, occasionally, changed the bed-linen—a thing which so exhausted me, that I was nearly in a fainting state before I was replaced in it. As I gradually became a little stronger, I bore the same with less exhaustion and inconvenience. Then her powerful assistance only was required, and I could sit, half-reclining, in the chair for eight or ten minutes. It was not, however, until some time after this, that I could raise myself in bed, or take any thing that was not put to my mouth; and it was still longer before I could sit up in bed without assistance. Then I came to be able to sit in bed in a semi-recumbent position, propped up with pillows,[1] for a short time, or until I became fatigued. At first this did not exceed a quarter of an hour or twenty minutes daily; but soon I was able to bear the position with comfort for half an hour, or longer.

---

[1] There is an apparatus kept in hospitals to place behind a patient, so that he may sit or recline at any angle; but being usually of iron, and rather heavy and cumbrous, it is seldom used. I found pillows much more convenient and comfortable.

Then I came to be helped out of bed every afternoon or evening, and to sit, wrapped in blankets, in a semi-recumbent posture in the arm-chair beside my bed. At first, this too was only for a quarter of an hour or twenty minutes at a time; but as my strength increased the time was proportionately lengthened. It was now that, early one morning, the kind 'sister' of the ward came to my bedside, as usual, to enquire how I had passed the night, and then treated me to a few jokes on my lying there so long, instead of getting up and dressing, and amusing myself among the other patients of the ward. Her object was to raise my spirits, and at any other time I should have laughed at it; but owing to the weak and depressed state I was in, and my defective hearing, I misunderstood it, and thought she really meant what she said. I at first regarded it as very cruel, and was much cut up about it. Indeed, I actually began to entertain the idea of bribing some of the able-bodied patients to carry me down stairs, and to put me into a cab, in order to go home; a thing which, of course, was perfectly absurd, and, indeed, impossible in the state I was then in. When M—— came I told her all about it. The matter was instantly explained; and what had so lately almost moved me to tears, was at once seen to be intended as a piece of good-natured pleasantry, which now provoked a laugh—the first healthy one that had appeared on my face since I was brought into the hospital.

As soon as I began materially to improve, a species of hysterical attack came on at intervals, generally without any assignable cause, and even when my mind was occupied with some pleasant subject, or I was engaged in conversation. I would then sob and gasp convulsively for a space of time varying from a few minutes to a quarter of an hour, or even longer. At length a flood of tears would burst forth, and immediate relief followed. Then I used to upbraid myself for my seemingly childish weakness, and feel ashamed at what had occurred; but in truth, I could neither help it, nor discover its cause. One of the surgeons said it arose from the debilitated state I was in, and that it was not an uncommon symptom. In two or three cases it occurred soon after my wife had left me for the night; and then, but not till after its accession, a feeling of my utter loneliness, helplessness, and dependence on others, would creep over me. Then my usual spirit failed me, and 'misgivings of the heart' would come on against my will. Then the conviction "My days are passed, my purposes are broken off, even the thoughts of my heart," would take possession of my mind; and the recollections of intentions frustrated, losses sustained, hopes and prospects destroyed, and the future darkened by this unfortunate accident, would, for a time, nearly overwhelm me, and was only relieved by sleep.

A little before this time M—— commenced reading a portion of Scripture to me daily, and from various books she brought with her; a practice which she continued until I was subsequently able to do so for myself. Then she would mark appropriate passages for me to read, and bring me books either of her own, or which she selected from the library, which she thought would amuse me, and which she deemed appropriate to one in the state I was in.[1] During more than half of the long time I was in the hospital she was the only one who afforded me religious consolation; and she continued her ministrations until I left the building—faithful to the last.

My sight was now so far restored, that, as I lay upon my

[1] There is either a Bible or Testament, and usually a Prayer-book, kept on the table at the side of every patient's bed.

back, I could see to read any thing printed in clear, bold type, by holding it in my left hand at some distance from my eyes. This was a great comfort to me; but at first, Mr. T——, my surgeon, objected to my indulging myself in this luxury; as he assured me it would prove injurious to my head. However, I could not wholly give it up; but limited my indulgence in it to, at first, only a short time daily. As my strength increased I read more and more, until reading occupied a considerable portion of my time, and proved a continual source of enjoyment to me. I was soon amply supplied with books from the library of the ward,[1] and others were brought me either by or through M——, and I could have the daily and weekly newspapers, whenever I liked to send for them. Of the last there was generally an abundance in the ward, as many of the patients received some of them from their friends, whilst others sent out and purchased them at the nearest news-shop.

My progress continued, and by-and-by I essayed to walk. My first attempt was a laughable one. It was like the tottering of an infant when it leaves its mother's knee. I crept out of bed, and, by holding to the side of it, managed to reach the bottom of it in safety. My ambition now was to walk, undressed as I of course was, from the foot to the top of it. I got along rather more than half the distance in safety, and then tottered and fell on my injured arm and shoulder across the iron-side of it, by which I shook and hurt myself very much. M——, and two or three of my fellow-patients who were near, immediately rushed to my

---

[1] Each floor or connected set of wards, in all our large hospitals, has a small, but usually excellent library of moral and instructive books attached to it for the use of the patients, including tales, histories, natural histories, travels, sermons, evidences of Christianity, the New Testament in the Latin vulgate, and in all the modern languages of Europe, &c., &c.

assistance, and I was soon in bed again. Nothing daunted, on the following day I again tried the experiment, and with comparative success. Two or three days later I got up, and after being dressed, managed, with the assistance of a person on each side of me, to reach the settee by the fire, where I sat for about an hour, when, with similar help, I regained my bed in safety. The fatigue of dressing and undressing, and of my long walk of some ten or twelve yards, appeared to do me good; for I fell into a quiet nap soon afterwards. I repeated my exploits, and for longer periods and distances daily, until my increasing strength and confidence enabled me to walk alone. In due time I became one of the regular walking-patients of the ward.

My time between meals, after rising in the morning, was now chiefly occupied in reading, in gossiping with the patients, in observing cases of interest and the changing scenes around me, and, as soon as I was able, occasionally assisting, in my turn, some bedridden or helpless brother-patient. Apart from the feelings which must necessarily attend a person in the situation I then was, I may say, that the time passed comfortably enough to prevent it hanging heavily on my hands. Indeed, the busy inner life of a large London hospital, and particularly the scenes and bustle of its accident-wards, afford ample materials to occupy the attention and to amuse any one of a cheerful temper and an observant mind. The new cases brought in alone continually cause excitement, and furnish subjects of interest to those already there.

I have not lately referred to visitors, wishing to avoid tedious repetitions; but the reader will no doubt infer from what I have said in previous chapters, that, during the long period just referred to, I had many of them, as heretofore. Two or three of them deserve a longer notice than I can give them. One of them was an eminent English surgeon whom I had the honour of knowing for many years, but whom I had not seen for some time. He had just returned from Paris, and hearing of my accident on his way home, kindly called at the hospital to see me. Owing to the state of my eyes I could not see his features, nor could I, at the instant, recall his name, although I recognised the voice as one familiar to me. On his leaving me I enquired his name; and then found that he had left for me, with M——, a splendid sponge-cake, which he had brought with him from France, hoping that I might be able to take a little of it dipped in wine.

Another of the gentlemen alluded to had been an old friend of mine, but I had lost sight of him for three or four years. His visit, however, did not take place until, though still confined to my bed, my sight had sufficiently returned to allow me to recognise him. On my telling him, with the assistance of M——, of the agony I had suffered, and still suffered, from the bed on which I lay, he kindly offered to send me down an invalid's water-bed, or air-bed—I now forget which it was—which he said he had at home. The worst part of my illness being over, and the hope of being soon able to leave my bed, led me to refuse this kind offer; a refusal, however, which I had afterwards reason to regret.

Another of the visits I received, and the last one to which I shall refer, was chiefly remarkable in being from one whom, of all the persons I had ever known, I should have least expected it. It was therefore the greater surprise, and the more acceptable to me.

About this time I received various little presents of fruit and flowers. The pale-eyed primrose and the sweet spring-violet were particularly acceptable to me; but the last was my favourite. I had the little bunch placed near me, so that I could see it continually, and reach it and smell it when I liked. I think if persons only knew how acceptable and refreshing such little presents are to a bedridden patient, they would be oftener led to make them. Well may the poet sing—

> "Blessed be God for flowers,—
> "For the bright, gentle, holy thoughts that breathe
> "From out their odorous beauty, like a wreath
> "Of sunshine on life's hours."

Notwithstanding that, regard being had to the state I was so recently in, my improvement might appear rapid, I continued in an extremely weak state, and had little more energy or power of taking care of myself than a child. My pulse was extremely slow and feeble, often to the extent of being scarcely perceptible. But what chiefly attracted notice and caused alarm was the state of my head. The scalp had receded to something approaching its natural dimensions, though still thick and spongy, but it refused to unite itself to the overlying membranes of the skull, and there was a distinct separation between them extending over a space larger than the whole under surface of my hand. It also continued to discharge copiously, and the wounds in it were still open—the latter, however, a fortunate circumstance whilst it continued in this state, as affording a place of exit for the discharge. The usual treatment—cold-water pads and tight bandages, with large poultices at intervals, as the symptoms indicated—had been tried, as before, in vain. The improvement was so little, that for a very long time it was scarcely perceptible. The wound in the side of my head and throat not only refused to heal, but for weeks, at intervals, increased in malignity and poured forth a prodigious quantity of pus. Then it would exhibit a more kindly character, and the discharge from it would lessen; but at the same time the glands of the throat would swell enormously and begin to suppurate, and my head would exhibit symptoms of renewed inflammation. It was then that the cold-water pads, or a portion of them, were exchanged for poultices, and vice versâ. This state continued, with little amelioration, until long after I had left the hospital; and even then, the improvement was so gradual that it was not until about eight months afterwards that I was able to wholly abandon the cold-water dressings. At this time I could, and sometimes did, insert my fingers between the scalp and the skull. The operation of dressing the wound in the side of my head and throat was particularly painful, especially whilst I was in the hospital, owing to the extreme tenderness of it and the surrounding parts. The pain produced by the pressure employed to force out *all* the matter in it was really agonising, and I could scarcely bear it.[1] And then the poultices and pads, unless frequently renewed, acquired such a degree of stiffness and hardness, that they also pained me, and often prevented my sleeping. From the difficulty of properly bandaging the part, the disturbing motion of the lower jaw, and my restlessness in bed, the pads and poultices would sometimes get displaced, and on awaking I have even found them lying beside me on the pillow.[2] The cold-water pads, owing to their nature, generally kept on better than the poultices. In general the whole of the side and back of my head up to the crown, including part of the throat, was covered with them; and, until latterly, the rest of the head with cotton-

[1] My own humble impression is that too much rough pressure is usually employed, in hospitals, in dressing sensitive tumours; and that the irritation thus set up often does much harm.

[2] If the very simple form of bandage for the head invented by one of the chief army-surgeons of the United States of America, and now in general use in their military hospitals, had been used, this could not have happened.

wool; the whole being retained in place by voluminous rollers or bandages enveloping the whole head, forehead, chin, and throat. These bandages were sometimes so artistically arranged by the nurse in reference to the forehead, face, and chin, that they gave me quite a romantic appearance; and some of my friends used to joke me by saying, that I looked like one of the old knights or Crusaders.

At length my improvement, notwithstanding the discouraging state of my head, led me to indulge the hope of shortly being sufficiently strong to bear removal home—home, with its many fond associations, on which my mind had so often wandered, and to which it still turned with delight and longing. A few days later, and I determined to leave the hospital the following week. But here again I was doomed to disappointment. A damp floor under me, and an unusually cold, damp day coming together, affected me greatly, and I suffered a short relapse. My appetite failed me, vertigo and shivering again came on, mist and muscæ volitantes again floated before my eyes, and my head suddenly grew worse. It was that horrid scrubbing-brush again, that had done the mischief. Happily the prompt attention paid me by Mr. T——, and his staff, restored me to my former state in a few days. On each recurrence of the 'scrubbing-day,' which is twice a week, I was afterwards careful to remove into an adjoining ward, and not to return to my own until the floor of the part of it where I was located, had become quite dry.[1] In this way I avoided the danger of another relapse.

[1] The practice of scrubbing the floors of sick-wards, though beneficial as an act of cleanliness, is not without its disadvantages, particularly in cases in which the patient is liable to suffer from exposure to damp. The 'dry-scrubbing' adopted in military hospitals is, in this respect, a much better method.

On one of the visits of Mr. H. H—— with his school of pupils, just after this, an incident occurred that was both amusing and instructive. Mr. M——, on removing the bandages to allow Mr. H—— to examine my head, in his haste slipped the pins that he took from it into his mouth. Whereupon Mr. H—— observing it, shouted out in his usual ready way, warning him never to do so again with pins taken from a bandage, as the danger was incalculable. The practice which some young surgeons have of putting pins into their mouth cannot be too strongly condemned, not merely for the reason named by Mr. H——, but also on account of the liability to swallow them on attempting suddenly to speak, an accident which I personally know has happened two or three times.[1]

On another visit of Mr. H. H——, and the last but one he paid the ward whilst I was an inmate of it, after looking at my head and observing on its obstinacy, he shook me by the arm, and remarked "Ah! I see that if that head of yours is not better by the time I come again, I must have another cut at it." This was, of course, a pure joke of his; but some persons who heard it thought otherwise. The truth is, that the previous incisions were still open, so that there could be no reason for making fresh ones; a fact which Mr. H—— had himself ascertained, by exploring them with a probe which he borrowed from one of his pupils.

And now the desire to get home once more seized upon me. I had become so extremely sensitive of the effects of damp and cold that I dreaded the slightest exposure to them. My house was dry, had a southern aspect, and

[1] The old system of sewing on bandages with needle-and-thread is now commonly replaced in hospitals by the use of pins. One or two pins suffice to secure a long bandage.

from its situation was entirely sheltered from cold winds. I flattered myself if I could only get there, I should soon become strong enough to take a little exercise in the garden during fine weather, and should then rapidly get on. This desire was strengthened by a disinclination to remain longer in the hospital than I could possibly help, as I might thus deprive some poor sufferer of a bed there who might perhaps need it more than I did. I was also reluctant to put the institution to expense by staying in it longer than I could possibly avoid. In this way my determination to leave the hospital within a few days was soon formed. An eminent surgeon of my acquaintance strongly advised me to go to the Convalescent Hospital for a short time, to recruit my strength before going home; and another professional friend offered to take me there in his carriage if I would go; but my mind had been previously made up. Although, from the state I was in, I was unfit to leave the hospital, home I must go, if I could possibly get there, at all hazards. I now began to prepare myself for my early departure; and requested my wife and family to make arrangements for my removal and reception home.

CHAPTER XII.

Inner-life of a hospital—day and night in the wards—morning—prayers—breakfast—physic—round of house-surgeon and staff—passing time away—rations, bread—noon—waiting for the pot-boy—porter, stout—dinner—visiting surgeons and physicians—leisure-hours—butter—milk—tea—evening—retiring to bed—night-scenes—dietary—medicines—dispensing, &c.—Sunday—operation-day—admission-day—discharge-day—preliminaries of departure, &c.

As soon as I had recovered my sight, every thing around me, every scene and incident, began to arrest my attention and become a subject of observation. As my eyes improved and I gained strength, besides being an attentive observer, I became highly interested in the affairs of the little community of which I formed a part. The situation of my bed was such that, although lying on my back in it, I could see not merely the whole of the ward I was in and the main portion of the next one, with every thing that occurred in them, but also the entrance to three others which could only be approached by passing through my ward. Thus, as the door to the whole was opposite to the foot of my bed, no one could pass, or be carried in or out, to any of the wards on that floor of the building, without my cognizance, so long as I was in a state capable of exercising it.[1] This was a great source of comfort to me, as it continually furnished fresh subjects to arrest my

[1] About eight or ten days before I left the hospital I was removed to the first bed in the immediately adjoining ward, to make room for an accident-case supposed to involve concussion of the brain. Here, however,

attention, and to occupy my mind, points of the utmost importance to a patient in the state I was in.[1]

To give the reader some further notion of the inner-life of a large London hospital than he can glean from the preceding chapters, I will endeavour to present him with a pen-and-ink sketch of an ordinary day and night in one of its large wards. We will suppose the time of the year to be between November and March, as some of the scenes I shall describe are then more characteristic than in the summer-season.

It is morning, early morning, for it is still dark. All is silent in the ward, unless the stertorous breathing of some heavy or fevered sleeper, or the occasional footsteps of the night-nurse, break in upon it. The bell in a neighbouring steeple tolls the hour of six. There is a movement in some of the beds—arms thrown about, or a change of position—indicating that it has partially aroused their inmates. Two or three may be now awake, or will shortly be so. Others are sunk in that heavy sleep or stupor which follows long pain, restlessness, or watching, or delirium, and will continue so for two or three hours longer, until the life and bustle near them arouse them from it. In another half-hour, perhaps, some patient more regardful of his personal appearance, or of cleanliness, than the rest, may be seen sitting up in his bed brushing or adjusting his hair, or assiduously polishing his teeth with a brush, anxious to seize the opportunity of doing so when he will be neither disturbed nor observed by those around him.

---

from the opening between the two extending through about half the space of the wall dividing them, I had a position nearly as good as the first one for observing what passed. Besides, at this time, as before, I passed greater part of the day in the accident-ward.

[1] See *pages* 175, &c.; also *Notes* p. 175-6, et infrà.

Soon, now and then, may be seen a gaunt and ghost-like form very sparingly robed in white, flitting or hobbling along, and suddenly disappearing through some side-door on a nameless errand; or returning from it, in like manner, to his bed. Presently, first one and then another of the patients may be seen sitting up in bed, or at the side of it, dressing.[1] Seven o'clock strikes, and soon after the day-nurses, one by one, come on duty. Now the patients who are up, or awake, may be heard talking to each other, or chatting with the nurse; or they may be seen dressing or washing, or busying themselves with other duties connected with their sparing toilet; or, perhaps, carrying bowls of water to others who wish to follow their example.

At half-past seven or eight o'clock—according to the season—Morning Prayer is read in each ward by the Chaplain, or, in his absence, by the matron or 'sister' of the ward.

Soon after this, most of the walking-patients of the ward whose state will permit it, are up and about, some of them busy washing, &c.; others, preparing for breakfast. Now an amusing scene commences. Those who are able to do so are seen hastening to the fire-place, tea-pot in hand, to obtain boiling-water for themselves, or for any fellow-patient in whom they feel interested, and who may not be able to rise so early, or to do it for himself.[2] Next one of the nurses passes round the ward with a tray or board covered with little jugs containing milk, one of which she deposits on the table or whatnot at the side of each patient's bed on her way.[3] Then the business of break-

---

[1] Working-men and country-people from being accustomed to rise early generally continue the practice when in a hospital, and are usually up before the other patients.

[2], [3] See *Notes*, pages 187, 188, &c., infrà.

fast commences. Sitting up in bed, or at the side of it, or on stools near their tables, all the patients who are able to do so, are soon deeply engaged in it. Two or three may avail themselves of a form, and sit at the centre table for the purpose. It now really does one good to see the relish with which the cups of tea are quaffed by nearly all the patients then patronising them, and the heartiness with which the food is taken by some of them.

It is now probably eight o'clock, or a little later. About this time, certain preliminary duties having been finished, the nurses commence attending to the breakfasts of their respective bedridden and helpless patients, and such who are unable to rise until a later hour. The tea is made, poured out, and, when cool enough, handed to the patient, and generally proves most acceptable to him. Perhaps an egg is beaten up with each cup of tea, or one of them; or it is accompanied with a little toast or bread-and-butter, as the case may be. In certain cases the whole of this is replaced by some other form of refreshment, either then or afterwards, as in my own early days in the hospital.[1]

The breakfasts being over, the nurse, armed with a towel and a large basin of hot water, goes through her department and, after washing the tea-service of each of her patients, replaces it in the drawer of his table, or on the shelf of his whatnot. Now the brooms are fetched from the wash-house or an adjoining closet, and the whole floor of the ward swept perfectly clean, particularly around and under

---

[1] The 'tea-pot system' is not found in all our large hospitals. In some of them the tea is provided and made, both in the morning and afternoon, by the 'sister,' or one of the nurses, and then served round in cups or basins to the patients—an excellent plan, much to be commended, particularly in the case of the poorer patients. See *Note*, page 195.

the patients' beds.¹ Then it is the duty of each nurse to visit her respective patients that require it with a basin of warm water, soap, towel, &c., and to wash them, comb and arrange their hair, attend to their dressings, &c., as the case may be, and has been noticed in a previous chapter. Next comes the making of the beds,² changing the linen, &c., with other matters of a similar kind. The floor, the beds, and the patients, having thus been rendered as clean and tidy as possible, the ward is ready for the morning visit of the house-surgeon and his staff.

About this time one of the nurses appointed by the 'sister' for the purpose, or the 'sister' herself, carrying a medicine-glass graduated into tea-spoonfuls and table-spoonfuls, with a basin of clean water to wash it in after use, proceeds round the ward, or set of wards, and administers to each patient the proper dose of the medicine standing on his table, as indicated by the label on it. This visit and physicking is repeated, in a similar manner, in the afternoon and evening.³

It is now (say) about ten o'clock. The nurses, or the patients themselves, have loosened or arranged the dressings, &c., ready for the coming inspection. One or two

¹ In this and the preceding duty, as well as in all similar ones, the nurses are commonly assisted by one, or more, of the convalescent or able-bodied patients, who feel happy thus to engage themselves.

² See *Note*, suprà.

³ The patients generally are rather anxious than otherwise to take their medicine, even when nauseous, no doubt thinking that it will do them good. There is only one sort that they frequently object to take a second dose of, and that is what is called in hospital-parlance '*house-medicine*.' It is a rather active kind of 'black-draught,' much disposed to act roughly in the very large doses which the nurses commonly give; and being usually strongly flavoured with peppermint is very apt to rise in the stomach. The older patients, who are "up to it," as they say, always manage to avoid taking it.

poor fellows may be seen sitting up in bed, or at the side of it, dressing the stump of a leg, thigh, or arm, which has been amputated, and has not yet healed. In a short time some of the 'dressers'[1] make their appearance, followed soon afterwards by the house-surgeon, the assistant house-surgeon,[2] and the junior members of the surgical staff of the hospital.[3] The round of the ward now commences, each surgical patient is visited in succession, and his case attended to, and directions given, as already noticed elsewhere. If any thing important or difficult is required to be done, the house-surgeon (or his chief assistant) usually does it himself in the presence of, and assisted by, his staff. Minor details, as the application or renewal of dressings, bandages, &c., which present no difficulty, are generally left to the dressers, or one of them, and the nurse, to attend to after the house-surgeon has left the bed. In this way half an hour, or an hour, may be consumed, acccording to the number and character of the surgical cases in the ward.

Now those patients who are able to do so, begin to amuse themselves, or pass their time, in various ways, according to their respective tastes. Those who have the permission registered on their bed-tickets, if the weather be fine, now prepare to take their walk, and soon disappear. Some occupy themselves in reading newspapers or periodicals, or books taken from the library of the ward. Others, in gossiping, or joking, in which one or other of the nurses usually comes in for her full share of harmless banter or

[1] Senior students appointed to perform minor surgical duties, as dressing, bandaging, &c., under the direction of the house-surgeon or his assistant.

[2] When not engaged elsewhere.

[3] In very large hospitals where there is more than one full house-surgeon, the wards are commonly divided between them; or some other arrangement is made to prevent their clashing in their duties.

raillery. Some are talking on a new case, or cases, brought in during the night, or are passing opinions and hazarding conjectures on the progress or termination of this or that case that attracts their interest, and respecting which, although they do not think so, they are supremely ignorant. In cold weather the neighbourhood of the fire-place seems to be the favourite resort of those able to reach it. The settees or forms stretching from its sides are usually well occupied, and every available stool or other seat brought into requisition around the front of it. Two or three of the more lively and agile patients are, perhaps, indulging in some merry frolics or capers in the central open space of the ward, taking care to desist as soon as they hear the footsteps of the 'sister' approaching. Others may be seen and heard hobbling or stumping about the wards on crutches or with sticks; perhaps one of them with a wooden leg. One or two of the humbler patients may probably be seen at the large centre-table peeling a huge bowl of potatoes, or conveying them in their finished state to the kitchen, in order that they may be dressed for dinner. At the end of the same table perhaps may be seen two or three patiently stretching and rolling up tight a lot of clean rollers or bandages, ready for use, by means of the little machine kept for the purpose. Then a couple of the able-bodied patients are seen returning from the steward's room with an enormous basketful of loaves of bread, which they deposit on some central, convenient part of the floor, near the 'sister's room.' In a short time one of the nurses, or one of the patients acting for her, is seen going round with a tray or board covered with bread consisting of the halves or quarters into which the loaves have been divided, and depositing one of them on the table of each patient as she passes it—it is intended for his day's supply.[1] Then some of the patients may be seen busy washing out their jugs, looking them up if missing, or otherwise getting them ready, as if in expectation of something shortly to be put into them. A good deal of uneasiness and restlessness appears to follow among a portion of them. Enquiries as to the time, the straining of eyes through one of the windows in order to catch a sight of the clock of a neighbouring church, the pulling out and looking at watches, &c., &c., are now noticeable occurrences. Then the remark that "the pot-boy is late this morning," may be heard, perhaps with the occasional additions "I am *so* thirsty," "I am really *longing* for my beer," &c. At about twelve, or a little earlier or later, that long-expected and important personage the pot-man or pot-boy arrives with two very large tin-cans of beer, having a pewter-pot hanging from the spout of each, and the whole polished like silver. His progress from the door to the centre table on or near which he deposits his burthen, is watched by several eager eyes, and a perceptible stir and excitement may be noticed among some of the patients. Then 'sister' makes her appearance, and, taking up one of the pint-pots, measures out each patient's share, and pours it into one of the jugs which, by this time, are collected on the table. Then comes the distribution of the filled jugs, which is done by the nurses assisted by one or more of the patients, in the usual manner. Judging by the heavy draughts taken by the recipients of some of them, and the evident satisfaction the liquor gives them, it must be very grateful and refreshing; and hence, sometimes, little is left to wash down the dinner, as is intended. The bustle and excitement thus

[1] It is, I believe, usually one of the halves of a 2 *lb.* or half-quartern loaf.

occasioned however soon passes away, and gossiping, or reading, or walking or sitting about, or something else of the kind, is again resumed by the patients.

'Dinner-time' is now approaching. The quiet just alluded to does not, therefore, last long. Occasional glances are soon again seen turned toward the door, and it is evident that something more is shortly expected to be brought through it. One o'clock is drawing near. One of the nurses comes, and calling to or beckoning a couple of the able-bodied patients who like to busy themselves in these matters to follow her, takes her departure for the kitchen down stairs. Now a number of the patients, and particularly the convalescents, are evidently on the qui vive for their dinners. Presently there are sounds of footsteps heard on the stairs, savoury fumes of viands are perceptible, and many eyes are eagerly turned toward it. Then the parties that left just before are seen returning, bearing a large tray or shallow basket between them containing a huge piece of fine roast-beef, steaming hot, with baked potatoes; or an equally fine leg of mutton, the latter being sometimes roasted, and sometimes boiled, by way of a change.[1] Following them comes the nurse with a tray containing some small dish of meat, a dish of baked pudding, and perhaps one also of boiled potatoes. Behind the whole, or following soon after, probably comes one of the older patients of the boys' ward carrying a large brown jug or pitcher containing beef-tea—real strong nourishing stuff—for the use of those patients that are ordered to take it. Now the 'sister' again makes her appearance, and, armed with a carving-knife and fork, and assisted by a nurse,

---

[1] The roasted joint appeared to be the favourite with the majority of the patients; both were so nicely dressed that I could hardly decide between them.

commences filling the plates which she takes from the pile before her. Potatoes are added, with a little gravy and salt. The distribution commences as soon as a few of the plates are filled, and is done in the way already explained. Then follows the onslaught; and it is really amusing and refreshing to see it among some of the patients, and particularly the convalescents, whose appetite is nearly always good. The contents of most of the large plates disappear in a remarkably short space of time. Long before I could eat much of these things myself, I was delighted to see others around me thus enjoy themselves. During the latter part of my time in the hospital I formed one of them myself.[1] In this way the dinner is soon over, and the jugs of beer emptied.

After dinner comes the collection of the plates, and their removal into the adjoining scullery or wash-house. At the time of their removal the knife and fork of the patient is wiped clean by the nurse, and either left on the patient's table, or returned to his drawer. Brooms are next introduced, and the ward is swept scrupulously clean, as in the morning. The beds are then straightened, and made tidy,

---

[1] The only difference between us, I must candidly confess, was that I controlled myself, and did not indulge in the outward display which I have alluded to. Every thing, from the 'ward' I was in to the 'food' served in it, was remarkably clean, and did infinite credit to the matron or 'sister' who managed it. The kitchen, &c., was, as I was informed, also creditable in this respect. Accidents will, however, occasionally happen. I remember a laughable incident connected with it. I was discussing, with much relish, a plate of very nice hot roast-beef. Suddenly I discovered the leg of a cockroach in the gravy. I at once put down my knife and fork and pushed the plate aside. However, my appetite was so keen at the moment, that I reconsidered the matter; and, placing the offensive limb on the rim of the plate, recommenced and finished my dinner. At home such a discovery would have destroyed my appetite for the day.

and any litter about them removed. The ward is now ready for the reception of the visiting surgeon and physician of the day, who each comes regularly about his usual time, which is somewhere between half-past one and three o'clock.

Dinner being over, even the more lively patients sink into a state of quiet for a time.

Now one of the visiting or head surgeons or physicians of the hospital makes his appearance accompanied with his pupils or class,[1] and goes his round of the ward, visiting the patients on his 'list,' as noticed in an early chapter.[2] On his entering the ward each of his patients repairs to his bed, if not already there, and remains there until the surgeon or physician has seen him, when, as soon as decorum will permit, he may again leave it if he wishes to do so.[3] During these visits silence and order is rigidly enforced in the wards.

Two or three hours of leisure now follow, which, according to the state or disposition of the patient, is passed much in the same way as in the morning. Bedridden patients, and those disturbed at night by restlessness and watching, commonly fall into a nap and doze away an hour or two; a

[1] These are chiefly young gentlemen, students at the hospital, of the age of 18 or 20 to 22 years, with some others older.

[2] Lengthy 'cliniques' or clinical lectures on the cases deserving it are now generally reserved for the lecture-room; the professor generally confining himself to a few short remarks (if any) addressed to his pupils at the bedside of the patient.

[3] This is expected of every patient. Indeed, it is one of the standing rules of our hospitals that he should do so; and unless he complies with it he is passed over, and perhaps gets reprimanded afterwards. Sometimes a patient purposely avoids being seen, as when he expects something disagreeable to be done which he wishes to defer. In these cases slipping into another ward, or into the wash-house, &c., or some other like petty trick, is resorted to. The same is required on the morning visit of the house-surgeon; but it is not then so rigidly enforced.

thing which is also often foolishly indulged in by patients that do not require it.[1]

As the afternoon advances the butter-plates are collected, and the day's supply of butter distributed to the patients. A little later, and the same occurs with the milk for tea.

The boiler attached to the stove or grate, or the large kettle on the hob, next engages the attention of some of the patients, who are always anxious to keep them full, and often make sad messes in doing so, for which they get scolded by the nurses. Then comes extra attention to the fire, in which the poker—that characteristic favourite of every Englishman—is put into continual requisition. A little after four o'clock and some of the patients[2] begin to make preparations for tea; and ere long are seen waiting with their tea-pots at the fire, or passing up and down the ward with them, as at breakfast-time.[3] Others, including most of those patients who belong to a better class of society, do not usually begin to think of tea until five o'clock, or later. However, a cup of tea appears to be relished by all of them in their turn. It always proved very acceptable to me. The tea is commonly got through in a much quieter way than either the dinner or breakfast; and the patients choose the time at which they like to take it. The affair, as a whole, is managed and passes off in a similar

---

[1] I say "foolishly," because this indulgence often seriously interferes with the night's rest of the patient.

[2] Chiefly working men, who are accustomed to take tea very early.

[3] See *Note*, page 187, antè. I may here add to what is said there, that each patient, in most hospitals, is expected to provide his own tea-pot, cup-and-saucer, spoon, knife and fork, &c. However, if this is inconvenient, the 'sister' will supply him with them for a trifling fee to compensate for wear-and-tear. This fee is usually only 'one shilling' for the whole time the patient may be in the hospital.

way to the breakfast. It forms the last regular meal of the day.[1]

The evening is passed much in the same way as the leisure hours of the morning and afternoon; but oftener with the addition of pranks or frolics by some of the patients to diversify it; and usually there is more gossiping and loud talking than at other times of the day.

The hour of retiring to rest is very early in all hospitals —usually eight o'clock in winter, and a little later (say, nine) in summer. Before this time the patients who feel so disposed (and many do so) commonly make a sort of supper on the bread and butter in their drawers, or of something which their friends have sent them, when they are permitted to receive such presents. This is commonly washed down with a little milk-and-water or cold tea; or, and not infrequently, with a little beer or gin surreptitiously obtained from a neighbouring store, or a little wine or spirit sent them by their friends or presented to them on their visits. By or before half-past eight o'clock, in winter, every patient is expected to be in bed;[2] at which time at least one half the gas-lights are extinguished, and the remainder (usually only one in each ward) are turned down low. The exceptions are rare. The only licensed ones I met with occurred once a week, or fortnight, when the chaplain delivered what he called one of his "cottage-sermons"—and very excellent they were—or a 'popular lecture' on some subject which he thought would interest the patients, as the 'circulation of the blood,' 'physiology

---

[1] See the next paragraph but one.

[2] Many patients, and particularly convalescents, feel this regulation very oppressive. I did so myself. It really appears absurd to expect adults, well enough to stay up later, to go to bed at an hour suited only for children.

of digestion,' &c. On these occasions forms were brought and placed around the long centre-table, and the whole of the patients capable of attending invited from the men's wards. These sermons and lectures did not begin until eight or half-past eight o'clock, and generally occupied some twenty-five or thirty minutes, by which the patients were, of course, kept up beyond their usual time. Sometimes also, when the sister had her evening out—which was seldom—a little advantage would be taken of her absence by the patients. On these occasions a little group would collect round the fire, and enjoy themselves in various ways—telling tales or anecdotes, singing in an under-tone, &c. Indeed, on one occasion we had quite a vocal concert there. One thing particularly amused me; and that was the shifts of certain inveterate patrons of the 'weed' to get a 'smoke,' a thing interdicted in the wards of a hospital. The artifices resorted to, and the trouble taken, by more than one of them to indulge their propensity, was absolutely laughable. Having got somebody to bring them in two or three pipes and some tobacco, the parties alluded to, seizing such an opportunity as that referred to, would seat themselves at opposite corners of the fire-place, and holding the bowl of their pipes, just within the chimney and their mouths close to it, puff away with an amount of enjoyment and self-complacency that seemed almost enviable. By this ruse the smoke did not enter the ward, and their peccadillo escaped the detection of those from whom they wish to conceal it.

At nine, or half-past nine, the house surgeon passes through the wards to see that all is right, stopping here and there at the bed of any patient whose case particularly demands attention.

Soon after this one of the nurses whose duty it is to

wash and keep the rollers, bandages, &c., in order and ready for use, brings those she has washed and hangs them up to dry before the fire, which, during the colder portion of the year, is kept in all night.

The duties of the day-nurses are now over, unless any thing of a very important character happens to occupy one, or more of them, longer.

At ten the night-nurses[1] come on duty; and then the 'night' of a hospital may be fairly said to be fully set in. The way the night passes must, of course, depend on the nature of the cases at any given time in the ward, and in those closely connected with it. It may thus be a quiet one, or the contrary. Perhaps, there may be one or more delirious patients there, who may disturb or interrupt the repose of the others by their mutterings, chatter, or ravings. Perhaps, one or more serious cases of accident or sudden fit in the street may be brought in; and the surgeons, called up from their warm beds, may be busily engaged with the nurses round the unfortunate ones. Perhaps the chaplain, hastily summoned, may be heard administering the last consolations of religion to a dying patient; or his friends that have been sent for may be gathered weeping round his bed; or, perhaps, there may be no other witness of his ravings, or his quiet death, than the night-nurse and such of his fellow-patients who may happen to be awake at the time—perhaps, not even these. So varied and uncertain is the inner life of a hospital, that one or all of these things may happen at any time, in a single night. At a

[1] Motives of economy usually induce the employment of too few nurses, and particularly night-nurses, in hospitals. Thus in the one of which I was an inmate there was only one night-nurse for the whole floor of the men's wards, embracing fifty beds. It was only on extraordinary occasions that she had any one to assist her. For some further remarks on "*Nurses*" see the *Appendix*.

time when all is quiet, and the staff of the institution and the patients are congratulating themselves on the agreeable fact, all may suddenly be disturbed, and bustle and excitement succeed.

And so the night in a hospital, oppressed with contingencies, passes away, and the morning again arrives—the time of the day at which I met the reader at the commencement of this chapter.

Some other matters connected with life in the wards of a hospital deserve a passing notice :—

The *dietary* of the patients in the large London hospitals, and I believe in others elsewhere, is most liberal and ample in all cases that require it to be so; and every thing entering into it is of excellent quality. It is divided into classes having reference to the requirements of the cases, one or other of which, as already stated, is ordered by entry on each patient's bed-ticket. 'Full diet,' which is the most prevailing one in the wards of a general hospital, usually consists of a liberal supply of fresh meat (8 or 10 *oz.* after being cooked), about 1 *lb.* of potatoes, 1 *lb.* of bread, a slice of pudding (on certain days), 1 pint of porter or stout, with butter and milk (to add to tea) in sufficient quantity for the tea and breakfast of any reasonable person —more of some of them than a patient, unless hearty, can consume.[1] The quantity of some of these, in the case of very hearty, hungry fellows recovering from accidents or operations, who have complained of it being insufficient to satisfy them, I have seen increased by one half, or even doubled, at the order of the surgeon. To promote the reparation of tissues, the union of fractures, &c., in addition

[1] Tea and sugar is, in this dietary, supposed to be found by the patient; but in some of the great hospitals, that is also supplied him. See *Notes*, page 187, 195, &c.

to the full diet with its beer, one or two pint bottles of XXX Dublin stout are often added; or a bottle of the best pale-ale to support the stomach and give tone to the system. To those patients for whom fermented liquors would be improper, a liberal supply of new milk is given; whilst in special cases requiring them, eggs, oysters, wine, brandy, or gin, and beef-tea, are provided, regard being had, not to the expense, but to the welfare of the patient.[1]

In reference to the *medicines* given to the 'in-patients,' I may remark that, in general, they too are of excellent quality, and, for the most part, well dispensed or made up; but the contrary is sometimes the case. It is the desire of the governors of these institutions that the best drugs and chemicals only should be employed, and the medical officers do all in their power to see that this is the case. The system of arranging for the supply of them by 'contract,' as is usually done, is not, however, one of the best to effect the object in view; and from it, occasionally, inferior samples of drugs and pharmaceuticals get into the dispensary.[2] Nor is the system by which the apothecary

---

[1] When the patient is able to look after the matter himself, his daily allowance of wine, spirit, or bottled-liquor, is sent to him every evening or morning; and, in helpless cases, is left on his table in charge of the nurse. Occasionally it happens that a patient cannot be trusted in this way, in which case the 'sister' keeps back the liquor until the time at which it is to be taken.

[2] I had no reason to complain of my medicines until about the third week before I left the hospital. At this time every thing connected with the dispensary-department appeared to go wrong. Putrid infusion of calumba with lumps of green mould floating on it was then several times supplied to me and other patients for quinine-mixture; and as we could not take it, we were compelled to throw it away. On two different occasions we were kept, for the whole twenty-four hours, altogether without medicine, owing to the absence of the dispenser; and on two or three occasions I only obtained it

or dispenser is usually elected one to always ensure a skilful, efficient, and steady man. Hence it is that I have known several instances of parties utterly unqualified either by skill or experience, or moral character, obtaining the office, to the annoyance of the medical staff, and the detriment of the patients.[1] The practice of allowing inexperienced pupils to dispense medicines, is also objectionable and dangerous.

In reference to the medicines supplied the out-patients, I will merely remark, that the crowding, hurry, and confusion, resulting from the presence of so many applicants at once, is a constant source of loose and careless dispensing; and, not infrequently, of mistakes which are sometimes serious.[2] It is doubtless very difficult to provide a remedy

through the kindness of Mr. M——, the assistant house-surgeon, who seeing my mixture-bottle empty, went and prepared a fresh batch of the medicine himself. This state of things arose, as I was told, from the personal affairs of the dispenser leading him to absent himself.

[1] I once knew a man who had been a gentleman's servant elected, by interest, to the office of dispenser. He was so ignorant of his business, that I personally heard him order 14 lb. of rock-salt for sal-ammoniac, and afterwards ascertained that he actually used to dispense the one for the other in making up collyria (eye-waters or eye-lotions), believing them to be the same. Another I met with, was so careless that he dispensed even such poisons as prussic acid, corrosive sublimate, &c., when in haste, without either weighing or measuring them, merely by guess-work. I could multiply instances.

[2] Errors in affixing labels not infrequently occur. On one of my visits to one of our largest hospitals, a female with all the symptoms of lead-poisoning was brought there in a cab. As an out-patient, a bottle of mixture and a bottle of lotion had been given her about two hours previously. It appeared, on examining the two bottles which had been brought back with her in the cab, that they had been accidentally mislabelled. The consequence was that the poor woman had washed her leg with the tonic mixture, and taken, per mouth, the poisonous lotion. By the use of the stomach-pump and appropriate antidotes, she was, however, fortunately "put to rights;" and in a couple of hours was able to return home.

for the evils complained of. To do so the whole system must be changed, which would be a great boon both to the medical officers and their patients.

The preceding remarks refer chiefly to 'daily life' in the wards of a large hospital; but there are other matters connected with them, that do not occur *every* day. In extension of what I have said in the earlier chapters of this little work, I will add a few more words on some particulars there merely alluded to, that may interest the reader.

Two days a week (usually only two) are what, in the wards, are technically called *visiting-days* (say, Wednesday and Sunday). On other days of the week the friends of a patient, as a rule, are only admitted to see him on presenting a governor's order, or by the courtesy of the house-surgeon or assistant house-surgeon. The hours of admission are commonly from two till four. During these hours, owing to numbers of visitors, the wards present a very lively appearance, and the patients to whom they come generally appear in excellent spirits. This is particularly the case on Sundays, when the wards, in their semi-crowded state, resemble some minor exhibition or fancy-fair. The scenes there at these times may be imagined. Presents are brought, fruit and flowers abound, there is much sitting on the sides of beds and gossipping, much passing to and fro, and many welcomes and adieus.

The *Sabbath*, apart from the hours that 'visitors' are there, is usually a quiet day in the wards. Its quiet, however, is not infrequently disturbed by the arrival of some accident-case, or, sometimes, by a death—for accidents and death have no respect to days. Once during the day service in the chapel is performed by the chaplain, at which every patient who is able to do so is expected to attend. There are also usually one or more benevolent and religious persons who pass through the wards during the afternoon or evening, conversing here and there on religious subjects with a patient, and distributing tracts and the like.

At every large hospital there is one day of the week on which operations are more particularly performed, and which hence is known as '*operation-day*.'[1] This day, at the hospital of which I was an inmate, was Saturday; and the time at which the operations commenced, two o'clock. Its approach is always looked for with interest in the surgical wards of a hospital. This interest increases as the day arrives, particularly among those patients who are about to undergo operations; but these parties seldom exhibit that anxiety and dread which persons unacquainted with hospital-life might be led to expect.[2] Except in pressing cases, operations are not performed until this day arrives; and in many cases, one, two, or even three operation-days, are allowed to pass over after a patient's arrival, before he is operated on. The object of the surgeon, in these instances, is to render himself perfectly familiar with the cases, and to bring up the health of the patient to a state as favourable as possible under the circumstances.[3] In some cases, as deformities, the operation is continued or repeated from week to week. The dinners of the patients about to undergo operations are kept back until after they are performed, as a full stomach at such a time would be dangerous, or at least injurious. Few of them, in serious cases, on their returning

[1] See *pages* 21-4; also *chap*. xiii, &c.

[2] I have, however, known two or three instances of patients 'shirking' an operation, by absenting themselves at the time it was to take place.

[3] That is "fatten them up for slaughter;" as an eminent operative surgeon at one of our great hospitals once jocosely remarked to me. To which he added, "You know we try to make every thing as pleasant, and as little hazardous to the poor creatures, as possible."

to the ward from the table of the operating theatre, are able to take it. Many that I have seen leave the ward in good spirits, I have also seen brought back to it in a state of prostration that has continued for some time; and now and then it does happen with one of them, that the dinner of the previous day is, alas! the last one he will take.

The weekly day for the general admission and discharge of patients, known in hospital-parlance as *admission-day* or *discharge-day* (both occuring together), is also a day of bustle and interest in the wards. Of the former I have already spoken.[1] In reference to the latter I may remark, that the morning is usually occupied by the patients about to leave or be discharged, in making arrangements for their departure. Then the 'sister' collects the bed-tickets of the patients referred to, and takes or sends them down to the clerk's office, or to the board-room. At the proper hour, usually soon after dinner, she collects the patients together, and proceeds with them down to the hall or lobby outside the board-room door. Here the patients wait their turn —the females having precedence—to appear before the governors prior to their departure. Having been introduced into the board-room, their names are called over, and each is separately asked whether he is satisfied with the treatment he has received whilst in the hospital—whether his diet, &c., has been sufficient and satisfactory to him, the nurses, &c., done their duty—and whether he has any complaint to make. If he or she has any complaint to make,

---

[1] See *page* 20, antè. There is one thing of interest to intending patients which I omitted to notice there: viz.,—That each ordinary patient must bring with him a change of linen on entering the hospital; and must pay for his washing himself, if his friends do not get it done. This does not, of course, refer to accident-patients; though these, subsequently to admission, are expected to be supplied with clean body-linen, if they can get it. See *page* 23, &c.

it is, at once, entertained and investigated. The answer from the patients, as far as my own experience extends, with only one exception, has always been "Yes!" to the three first questions; and "No!" to the last one.[1] Each patient is then expected to express his thanks to the governors and officers of the institution, through the chairman. The chaplain now hands each patient a small paper or ticket containing a printed form filled up with the name of the patient, and the date, which he requests him to give, or cause to be given, on the following Sabbath, to the clergyman or minister of the church, or other place of worship, which he usually attends.[2] The patients now return to their respective wards, from which they take their departure either at once, or within a few hours afterwards.[3]

In the next chapter I shall say a few words about my fellow-patients and their cases.

[1] The exception referred to—a rare one—was that of an ill-conditioned fellow, whose complaint, on investigation, was found groundless. I have heard of, but have not personally known, one or two other like cases.

[2] This ticket simply expresses the desire of its holder to return thanks to Almighty God for the cure or benefit which he has received during his residence in the hospital.

[3] Every patient is expected to comply with the above regulations. Refusal to thus attend the board-room, and previous ill-behaviour, preclude his receiving future benefits from the institution, unless in the case of an accident. However, owing to the awkwardness of the affair when an applicant comes armed with a "recommendation" from a subscriber or donor, it is only rigidly carried out in very bad cases. The subsequent use of the chaplain's ticket is, of course, optional.

CHAPTER XIII.

Subject continued—ward-scenes—fellow-patients—interesting cases, accident-, surgical, and medical—operations—deaths, &c.

OF my fellow-patients in the hospital, and their cases, I could easily fill a volume, so numerous and varied are the materials which they furnish, both for narrative and remark. My space will, however, only permit me to briefly notice a few of them.

The festive season of the year about Christmas, particularly the first half of the month of January, is generally prolific in cases of 'delirium tremens' or drunkards' madness. In my earlier days in the hospital there were several of them, with the usual painful and fatal scenes that accompany them. It is always painful, indeed horrible, to see or hear a being formed in the divine image of his maker, acting and raving like a madman to a degree that renders it compulsory to have recourse to physical restraint to keep him in bed, or to prevent his doing violence to himself and others;[1] and this is particularly so when, as in the case of delirium tremens, the calamity is brought on the patient by that most disgraceful and degrading of all vices—habitual drunkenness. Notwithstanding that the usual precautions were adopted, one of the patients, almost in a state of nudity, attempted to escape from the hospital, and was not arrested in his progress until he had nearly passed the stairs leading into the hall of the building. There were two or

[1] In bad cases it is even necessary to restrain the patient with a strait-waistcoat, and by strapping him down in bed.

three deaths among them. One was a particularly painful case. It was that of a man who, as it was stated, had spent the ten days or fortnight following Christmas-day in continued heavy drinking. At last, being in a public-house, he made the foolish and often fatal bet, that he would drink a certain enormous quantity of gin[1] without rising from his seat. He had nearly accomplished the horrible task which he had voluntarily undertaken, when he fell senseless to the floor. He was conveyed to the hospital, and every thing was done for him that professional skill could suggest, and that the resources of the institution could provide. I believe that he was restored to consciousness after a time; but the state he was in almost precluded the hope of his recovery. Every thing that was administered to him was immediately ejected with convulsive violence. He lingered in a dreadful state until about the tenth day after his admission, when he died—died as much a suicide as if he had taken arsenic, or had cut his throat with a razor.

Among *accident-cases* I may mention one that was particularly distressing, and that rapidly proved fatal. It was that of a middle-aged man run over by a Hansom cab. The poor fellow had been discharged from St. George's Hospital only on the previous Saturday. He had been under treatment for an accident to his ankle, but had perfectly recovered from it. On the Tuesday, he was knocked down and run over, one of the wheels passing from the thighs across the abdomen. He was admitted late in the day. The abdomen and its contained viscera were all more or less seriously injured; and, I believe, the bladder was ruptured. Some slight operation was at once necessary to relieve the last. Inflammatory symptoms soon followed the injuries, and surgical skill could not prevent

[1] Twenty-four half-quarterns. Some parties stated it was more.

gangrene setting in. The second night he was delirious, and it was evident that he could not survive long. The chaplain attended him a little before midnight; and, after talking to him on his condition, read at his bedside the appropriate service of the "Book of Common Prayer." His wife was sent for, and, after seeing him, remained for the rest of the night by the fire in an adjoining ward, so as to be on the spot. The surgeons attended him frequently during the night, and the nurse was ordered to sit by him and watch him. His ravings and expressions of agony were dreadful, and disturbed the whole ward. Informed of his danger and awakened to a sense of his sins by the chaplain, he kept wildly calling on that God and Christ to relieve his sufferings and to save him, that he had rejected whilst in health. But he survived the night. The next day he was easier; and for hours, at intervals, appeared free from severe pain. He seemed to have quite forgotten the horrors and warnings of the night, and occasionally even conversed cheerfully with the nurse and some of the patients. His bed was opposite to mine, and not far from it. My eyes continually rested on him. At about seven in the evening he was swearing at one of the boy-patients for not tying the band that kept the wash-house-door near him partly open, and stretched forth his arms to show him how to do it. In another hour the delirium returned, and soon the scenes of the preceding night were repeated in an aggravated form. The dying man even sat up in bed and raved. The surgeons scarcely left him now. About four o'clock he became a little quieter. Then he ceased to speak; and, as he had lived, he died.[1] His wife was called

---

[1] This case afforded another instance of the pain often caused by the application of ice. The bladders containing it were constantly thrust off immediately the surgeon's back was turned. Such acts are common.

to see him, and then returned to her seat at the fire. In a short time the nurses performed their unpleasant duties on the corpse; and then, decently bound up, or dressed in a sheet as a shroud, it was placed in the 'black-box' or hospital-coffin and borne to the dead-house, there to await a coroner's inquest.[1]

In contrast to the above painful case I will mention another accident-case, the patient occupying the very next bed to the last one. It was that of Charles B———, one of the men engaged in removing the houses in the Strand on the site of which the new Railway Hotel was afterwards built. The lofty wall on which he was engaged with his pick-axe suddenly fell, and he was buried beneath the ruins. On being dug out, he was conveyed to the hospital—the nearest one. His fellow-labourers before doing so, offered him some spirit, and pressed him to take it, to revive and support him; but though he had no objection to liquor at other times, he resolutely refused it now. On examination it was found that his collar-bone was broken, his left hand crushed, his head cut open, and his back over the left scapula much injured, besides numerous bruises. He turned out to be one of the finest specimens of an English working-man I ever saw. Somewhat above the middle height, firmly built, admirably proportioned, and with a skin as white and delicate as that of a woman, he would have formed an admirable model for the painter or sculptor. His intelligence, ready wit, amiable temper, kind and obliging disposition, and decorous language and behaviour, soon made him a favourite in the ward; and I am happy to say that he maintained his good character, without a single

[1] There is always an Inquest held on the bodies of accident-patients that die in the hospital, as elsewhere; but not on the bodies of those that die under or in consequence of operations.

flaw that I heard of, until he left the hospital. The constitution of this man was so remarkably strong, that notwithstanding the nature of his injuries, neither erysipelas nor any awkward symptoms came on. His wounds assumed a healthy appearance, and might be said to have healed almost with the 'first intention.'[1] I was startled to see him get out of bed on the second day after he was brought in, and, after some struggling with his uninjured arm and hand, get on his trousers, and then leave his bed for a few minutes. In about nine or ten days he became one of the regular walking-patients of the ward.

Then there was a young man lying in the next bed to me with a very badly crushed hand. He was a book-binder by trade, and the accident had arisen, I believe, by his hand being drawn between the cylinders of one of the presses. For a long time he was kept a bed-lier (although able to rise), and on full diet with bottled stout, for the surgical motive of raising the tone of the system, and promoting healthy action in the injured part. He ultimately escaped with only the loss of the first joint of one or two of the fingers, from caries. He was a very respectable well-conducted fellow, and also deserves praise.

After him the same bed was occupied by a fine young fellow, of about twenty or twenty-one years of age, with a broken leg. His case was remarkable chiefly from his not knowing how it was done. He and some of his acquaintances were frolicking together, and, in chasing one of them, he suddenly fell and found his leg was broken, although it had not struck against any thing.[2] He was a lively young

[1] That is, rapidly, without supervenient inflammation or suppuration.
[2] This reminds me of a case I heard related by Mr. H. H——, my surgeon. A respectably attired man was found, (I think) one morning, lying on the grass in one of our public parks, at some distance from the

man, despite the tears he at first usually shed at night at being thus situated far away from home, and from a mother that he often talked of, and appeared to much love and respect. I observed that not a day passed without his reading some chapters in the Bible provided for him on his table; and he was also fond of reading the books brought him by those who visited him, or supplied from the library.

Then there was a man with the most extraordinary finger I ever saw. He was in a large way of business as a French polisher. The history of his case is singular. This man was a very respectable and sensible fellow, a very pleasant companion in his way, and an excellent singer. The latter qualities made him a general favourite among his acquaintances. This led him into company and habits which he found injurious to his business, and, to remedy the evil, he became a Teetotaler. The change was too sudden and extreme; his health became seriously affected, and, before long, very delicate. At this time he had a slight scratch on his finger, and the French polish got into it—an accident which, under ordinary circumstances, would have produced no inconvenience. In his debilitated state, however, the effects rapidly became serious. The slight wound grew painful and exhibited symptoms of being poisoned; and ere long the finger had swollen to a prodigious size, the swelling also involving a portion of the hand. The patient was immediately put on full-diet with a liberal allowance of bottled XXX.; and the finger was deeply incised longitudinally throughout its full length, both in the upper and under

carriage-way, with his legs broken near the ankles, and other injuries. On being roused, he could give no account of himself, or how the accident happened, or how he came there, though otherwise conscious; and what was strange, neither his clothes, nor the injured parts, exhibited any appearance that could elucidate the mystery.

surface. Cold-water dressings, and quiet, did the rest. The swelling declined, and the finger ultimately returned to its natural size; but the bone of the first joint became carious, and had to be removed with the forceps. This too is a case in lively contrast to the first one.[1]

The case that succeeded me in the bed from which I changed to another[2] furnishes a lesson that it would be well for some persons to read. The patient was a tradesman in a large way of business, and had the contract to keep in repair and order the gas-pipes, burners, &c., at one of our larger theatres. To guard against sudden emergencies, one or two of his men, and often himself as well, remained at the theatre until after the performance was over. On the occasion alluded to, he and a couple of his men left the theatre about one or two o'clock in the morning, in his spring-cart or trap, when, on their progress home, they "must needs" stop by the way to "have a drink." How long they stopped, or what they took, I do not know; but both may be inferred from what followed. The vehicle, with its occupants, either asleep or in a listless state, is afterwards seen proceeding through the Strand at a furious rate. The curb-stones are neared, a lamp-post is run against, the horse falls, and the persons in the vehicle are thrown out. All of them are more or less injured; and one of them is carried to the nearest hospital in a senseless state, his face and head covered with blood, and his features sadly battered and disfigured. Concussion of the brain is

[1] Mr. C——, the visiting-surgeon whose patient this man was, stated that when he was a student he had a similar finger, which arose from cutting himself whilst dissecting.

[2] See *page* 184, antè. [It is always usual to give serious cases one of the central or more airy beds in an accident or surgical ward. Such cases include broken thighs and legs, and all serious fractures, concussion of the brain, bad scalp-wounds, &c., &c.]

suspected. The next day partial consciousness returns. In a few days, being a well-to-do man, his friends come and fetch him home.

Within a few hours after the last patient had departed, the same bed was occupied by one of the hard-working porters of Covent-Garden Market. He was one of a train of porters carrying heavy crates of cabbages.[1] He treads on a piece of cabbage-stem in his way, slips, and falls. The loaded man behind him, unable to stop himself, falls too, the crate he carries falls on the other's legs, and breaks one of them.

The second or third bed from mine was, for some time, occupied by a man whose case was a particularly hard one. He had been for a great many years a waiter at a large and very respectable tavern and coffee-house in the neighbourhood. One night some drunken ruffians came in, and 'kicked up a row.' In attempting to restore order he was knocked down, and severely kicked with their heavy boots. The result, besides other injuries, was a fracture of the leg just above the ankle. He was a married man, with a family that did credit to him. He told M—— that he did not know what he should have done during his affliction, had he not always been a steady, prudent man, who regularly laid by a little "against a rainy day."

In the next bed to the one last noticed, was another very respectable man, the foreman, I believe, of the machine-department at a great neighbouring printing establishment. His hip had been injured by a blow from some part of the machinery.

Another large printing-establishment in the neighbourhood furnished us, soon after this, with a very melancholy case. It was that of a youth of about fifteen years of age.

---

[1] They weigh about 3 *cwt.* each.

He was under the inner part of the machine, and engaged in oiling the part on which the heavy bed runs. By some accident the machinery was suddenly set in motion whilst he was still there. He was sadly hit and cut about the face and head, and remained for a long time insensible. I observed him wince a little two or three times whilst the wounds were being sewed up, which were all the signs of pain which he exhibited. Poor fellow! As consciousness subsequently returned, the first words he uttered were " Mother! mother!"

Then there was a jobbing "tinker" brought in, an Irishman, who afforded the patients much merriment. He had, whilst in a drunken state, been pushed down by some passing vehicle, by which one of his feet and ankles was very slightly injured. After the removal of his nearly ragged clothing, the very filthy state he was in (not from the accident) compelled the nurse to thoroughly wash his skin from head to foot. During the operation he roared and groaned most lustily, like a looby boy, imagining he was being hurt—the other patients, able to do so, at the same time roaring with laughter. The next morning he was visited by his loving wife and a daughter; a visit that attracted some attention from one of them having a black eye, and the other her face somewhat disfigured by apparent violence. His case furnished another lesson on the degrading effects of drunkenness. He was a really intelligent, well-informed man, as I afterwards heard from his conversations with some of the patients, and had once been well off. Drink had reduced him to the state of poverty and degradation he then was in. In about eight or ten days afterwards he left the hospital perfectly cured, and in a cleaner and more creditable state generally than when he entered it.

A day or two later and another melancholy case was

brought in. The patient was a genteel young fellow, scarcely twenty years of age. He had been out for a Sunday's excursion. In returning, in the evening, he fell off the top of the omnibus, and one of his thighs was fractured. It will be a long time before he will be able to break the Sabbath again.

Among *surgical cases*, not accidents, I may mention that of a young man about twenty-two years of age. He had, from nearly his birth, a tumour in the throat, and another in the face, both of which, of late years, had gradually increased in size until they became large and annoying. I believe he also had some defect or absence of part of the bone of one of the eyebrows. He was robust and active, and, apart from the above, appeared in excellent health. I may add that he was the only and much-loved son of a widowed mother, and a lively, harmless, good-tempered fellow, fond of busying himself in the domestic duties of the ward, and also fond of reading serious books. He came into the hospital to have his tumours removed. After remaining there about a fortnight it was thought by his chief surgeon, Mr. H. H——, that he was in a fit state for the purpose. The operation-day—his last on earth—arrived. He was in particularly good spirits. He said they need not keep back his dinner, as he would not eat it until the operation was over. His fellow-patients joked him on the subject, and he joked them in return. A few minutes before he went to the operating theatre I saw him amusing himself in sweeping-up the ward. Half an hour afterwards he was brought down and placed in the next bed to mine. He was then still partially under the influence of chloroform. The hæmorrhage from the large blood-vessels of the throat was considerable; but was, after a time, temporarily arrested by the surgeons. For a short time we thought he was sleeping. Then came a sort of guttural cry for help, and I saw the blood spirting from his throat into the air like the jets of a fountain. Poor M——, who was at the time sitting between the head of his bed and mine, instantly called the nurses and 'sister.' The house-surgeons and several others then in the hospital were immediately on the spot, and assiduously laboured for about half an hour to stop the hæmorrhage. They seemed to have succeeded, a lull came, and they left him for some other case. A little time after this, and two or three gurgling groans escaped the poor fellow, and all was over. In about two and a half hours after he had left the ward, full of life and spirit, he lay in it a—corpse. Next came the sad final duties of the nurses. At night the 'shell' or hospital-coffin was brought, and the body was borne to the dead-house. Early the next morning—it was Sunday—there was the painful scene of a mother bewailing a lost son. The undertakers shortly after removed the body to his late home, preparatory to the funeral.[1] In a day or two this melancholy case ceased to be talked of, and appeared to be forgotten.

After this the second bed from mine was occupied by a hale, sprightly old man, with a cancer in the cheek, close to the edge of the mouth. He also had remained in the hospital for about a fortnight before he was operated on.

---

[1] See *Note* p. 209.

[2] A few hours after his death, Mr. T—— came to my bedside, and very kindly said that he hoped such an occurrence close to me had not alarmed or disturbed me. It had not. On the contrary, I had felt deeply interested in it, and had watched it closely. He also showed me the tumour that had been removed, and pointed out its nature. I had, however, seen it previously, one of the nurses having brought it to me for my inspection. I should say that it was about the size of a swan's egg.

The frightful spectacle the poor fellow presented after the operation, and until the long pins that held the wound together were removed, may be better imagined than described. I felt much interest in his case, and greatly sympathised with him on account of his age, and his not appearing to have any friends who cared for him. For a long time he remained in a very precarious state, in which he still was when I left. I afterwards learned that he ultimately rallied, and left the hospital cured.

Another operation that occurred whilst I was there, was one on the ankle-joint of a youth of about sixteen years of age. He had been in the hospital for some weeks under preparation for it. He also was a patient of Mr. H. H—— the eminent operative surgeon, who has invented a new mode of operating for deformity of the ankle, in which he has been particularly successful. I saw the lad carried on the back of one of the patients to the operating-theatre; and subsequently saw him, on his return, borne by three or four of the surgical staff to his bed. There was not much hæmorrhage after the wound was dressed. As he lay in bed still under the influence of the chloroform that had been administered, his features exhibited that peculiar paleness and placidity, almost angelic, that is characteristic of the action of this drug in such cases.[1] As its effects began gradually to wear off, the same placidity of features continued, but there was a plaintive expression combined with it, or seemed to underlie it, that indicated inward distress, or exhaustion; and the impression thus conveyed was increased by the vacancy observable in the eyes, and the ceaseless movements of the head from side to side. These appearances continued, in a diminished form, far into the

[1] In children, youth, and females, of agreeable or regular features, this is often very marked.

following day. I saw the joint the first time the bandages were removed to dress it. Its appearance fully indicated the fearful nature of the operation, as well as the consummate skill with which it had been executed. The youth progressed favourably up to the time at which I left the hospital, when I lost sight of him.[1]

The case of another youth, also between fifteen and sixteen, greatly interested me. His elbow-joint had been operated on, and the arm afterwards kept in one position, for weeks, by means of splints and bandages. It was then found to be semi-anchylosed, with the parts surrounding it in a corresponding state; and considerable force had to be employed to restore mobility to them. This, like the former operation, was done whilst the youth was under the influence of chloroform. The position of the joint was subsequently altered, at first every second or third day; and then, every day. The agony the poor fellow suffered while these changes of position were being made was painful to witness. He was, however, a good, bold boy, and latterly would often do it himself, grinning and groaning all the time, with his eyes streaming with tears.[2]

---

[1] Mr. H—— is celebrated for operations of this kind. There was a boy in the ward of about twelve, a shrewd, interesting, nimble, affectionate little fellow, who had been thus operated upon a few months before. Also another, older. The first had been in the hospital about nine months. His ankle had become strong and useful, but was not quite sound, as a little pus was still discharged in the neighbourhood of the wound formed by the operation.

[2] I cannot help noticing here the state of the youth and boys in what is called the "*boys' ward.*" Every thing was done to make them comfortable and happy. It was really pleasant to see them busily engaged in making purses, collars, &c., of beads, or in making toys, writing copies, reading, frolicking with each other, &c.; and, in the evening, playing at draughts or dominoes, or 'oughts and crosses' on their slates, or at setting each other puzzles. They appeared to thoroughly enjoy them-

Then there was a young man in the nearest corner of my ward, whose knees were permanently contracted and drawn up to his chest, who had his loins cauterised with caustic potassa daily, and for whom a tackle of ropes and pulleys for each leg was fitted to the bottom of his bed. It was, I believe, the result of neglected rheumatism or cold. He was now in a decline. He belonged to a respectable class of society, had many visitors, among whom were his parents; but what struck me as remarkable was, that neither his wife nor children were among them. He left the hospital soon after I did, little better than when he entered it. His case was a hopeless one.

Then there was a man from the country, a simple, good-hearted, honest fellow, with cancer of the nose, who escaped an operation by the skilful use of poultices and tannin, under the direction of the surgeons.[1]

And so of many other cases, each sui generis, deserving notice if my space permitted it.

The *medical cases* in the hospitals that attracted my attention, were nearly as numerous as the surgical ones; but I can only notice three or four of them here.

One of the beds next to mine, during my early days in the hospital, was occupied by a gentleman suffering from inveterate gout, and who left before I was able to see what was taking place around me. I name him chiefly on account

selves. The mutual affection of two or three of them was remarkable. I have seen the little fellow alluded to above, kissing and consoling another older than himself, after an operation, telling him how he himself had suffered the same, and how nicely, by patience, he had got over it; and sometimes even getting into bed and lying by his side to keep him company.

[1] Poultices of linseed-meal at night; and, in the day, an ointment or linement made by triturating tannin or tannic acid with just sufficient glycerine to give its form. Latterly, I believe, the ointment alone was used.

of the interest he took in me, and his kindness in repeating, at any hour of the day, or the night, my scarcely audible calls to the nurse.

In the same bed, some time afterwards, was Mr. G——, another gentleman who was most kind and attentive to me, and who, being up during the day and, apart from his peculiar affection, in good health, was able and always ready to assist me. He was a student in one of our public colleges, and was a young man of excellent education and parts, well acquainted with divinity, literature, and the current subjects of the day. As soon as I was capable of engaging in it, we often spent hours daily in conversation. The result of the acquaintance thus casually formed, was an attachment to him that still survives; and I trust, that not long after I left the hospital, he also left it restored to perfect and permanent health. He was a patient of Dr. W——'s. His disease was a peculiar one—ichthyosis[1]; but not a severe form of it. His treatment may appear curious to the non-medical reader; and some part of it, even amusing. It consisted essentially of warm baths, and, at least twice a day, vigorous friction with oil of cade ointment[2] or with a large piece of fat bacon to which the rind was left attached to hold it by, the two being commonly used alternately. The chief internal medicine was simple powders composed

---

[1] 'Fish-skin disease,' so named from the state and appearance of the cuticle. It commonly appears in patches, or on particular parts of the body. In the variety of it known as *ichthyosis cornea*, there are indurated excrescences, which, in exaggerated forms, somewhat resemble spikes, or even horns, when it is popularly called the '*porcupine disease.*' Persons so affected furnish the *porcupine-men* and *porcupine-boys* sometimes exhibited in shows at country fairs.

[2] *Unguentum Cadini.* Oil of Cade (*huile de Cade*) is the empyreumatic oil of the *juniperus oxycedrus* or *Languedoc juniper.* It resembles oil of tar, but is more aromatic.

of sulphur and cream of tartar. This was supported by the usual full-diet of the hospital supplemented with water-cresses, and with milk as a beverage instead of beer. Under this treatment my friend progressed wonderfully, and gained in flesh daily. In a few weeks he became quite stout, and was, as folks say, "the picture of health." Indeed, at last the fat appeared to actually ooze out of him, saturating his clothes, and even staining whatever he sat or lay on. I need scarcely add, that this led to many jokes being 'poked at him' by his fellow-patients.

At one time, nearly opposite to mine, was the bed of a poor fellow labouring under chronic bronchitis complicated with tuberculosis. He was a big, gaunt man, declining in life. The fare of the hospital, and the care taken of him, appeared luxuries to him. On his discharge "improved," thinly clad, without even flannel next his skin, and with the scanty and inappropriate diet and wretched accommodations of a very humble home, he had to contend with the cold weather of the winter. The reader may anticipate the consequences.

After my removal to my second bed,[1] shortly before I left the hospital, close beside me was a lad afflicted with leprosy. Next to him was a dear little fellow waiting to be operated on for contracted knee-joint which compelled him to walk with a crutch.[2]

---

[1] See page 184.

[2] The operation in this case, I believe, would be mere gradual extension of the limb, whilst the patient is under the influence of chloroform. It had been tried once without material success. One Friday I heard the little fellow ask Mr. C——, whose patient he was, to try it again next day. Mr. C—— told him he could not do so without first seeing his friends; and then inquired the residence of his parents. I name this to show the consideration and delicacy with which young patients are treated in our hospitals.

Next to the last named patient lay a French gentleman afflicted with a very severe form of bilious fever. He had been a merchant in an extensive way of business, at Paris; but, owing to some commercial misadventures, was then engaged in the hotel and wine business in London. The number of foreigners of a superior class who visited him, attested the position he had formerly held, and the respect and regard they they still had for him. As soon as evening came in he was attacked with delirium, which increased for hours; and, as usual in such cases, did not abate until early morning. His fluency at this time was remarkable; indeed, the rapidity with which he talked to himself, and held imaginary conversations with others, was wonderful. In the morning, on two or three occasions, he laboured under the delusion that the nurse had given him a 'good shaking' in the night to make him hold his tongue, and seriously complained of it. His case, for a time, appeared a rather hopeless one; but he ultimately rallied, and, as I heard, left the hospital two or three weeks after I did.

In the next bed to the French gentleman lay a poor young fellow of about twenty, in a 'decline,' as it is popularly called, gradually sinking and wasting away to a mere skeleton. He had then been there many weeks. Notwithstanding the extraordinary care and attention paid him, I heard that he died a few weeks after I left the place.

Just opposite my new bed, and not far from it, was the spot where the notorious Major M—— for some time lay after his bloody and murderous conflict in —— street, Strand; and in the immediately connected ward entered by the door on the left, was the spot where his victim, with his two-and-twenty wounds, lingered for a time, and died.[1]

---

[1] The particulars of the ruffianly and murderous 'duello' referred to, which took place in the privacy of a money-scrivener's office upstairs,

In a room or small ward[1] on the same floor, and closely adjoining the one in which I was located, lay a man advancing in life. He was Mr. S——, the once celebrated 'racing-prophet.' He could, and did occasionally, behave like a gentleman; but the profanity of his language, and the oaths and other expletives that disfigured almost every sentence which he uttered, and the continual threats which he indulged in, made him an object of either terror or disgust to the few patients that were in the same ward with him. The chaplain he utterly derided. Various persons attempted, at different times, to convince him of the folly and wickedness of his conduct, but in vain. Even ladies had kindly tried their influence on him for the purpose. M—— visited him several times under the pretence of enquiring after his health; but in reality to seize an oppor-

with no witnesses but the parties engaged in it, are doubtless remembered by the reader.

[1] The respective merits of 'small wards' and 'large wards,' or in other words, of 'rooms' and 'wards,' for the sick, have been much and angrily debated in the medical periodicals of late years. I fear that many of the disputants were practically unacquainted with either of them; and that none of them spoke on the subject from knowledge acquired by actual residence, as a patient, in a hospital. The utter desolation of a ward containing two, three, or even four beds, is horrible. There is no privacy. Every act is watched, and commented on; every thing disagreeable is doubly perceptible. In a large open ward it is very different. There each patient sees one or more like himself, and all feeling of diffidence is lost. He can meet with some others to mix and talk with—something to engage his attention, and to pass away the time; and more than all, fellow-patients who will be always ready to assist him, and at least one nurse always within call. The reverse of all this is the case in a very small ward. I have known patients beg to be removed, as a favour, to a small ward; but who, within a few days, have begged still harder to be allowed to return to their former one. It appears to me that a ward of from twelve to fifteen beds is the most comfortable and convenient. One with less than *ten*, or more than *eighteen* beds, is objectionable.

tunity of speaking to him on serious matters, and awakening him to the sense of the danger he was in. He was always civil and polite to her; as, indeed, he generally was to ladies. On one occasion he admitted to her that he knew his language and conduct were wrong, but he "could not help it"—it was "his way"—he was not "going to die yet," and—he did not "see much harm in it after all." Strange! but this man was visited continually by persons professedly gentlemen, even, as I was told, by persons of noble birth; but who, one and all, were 'sporting characters' who either sought his opinions on racing matters, or recollected previous services of the kind he had rendered them. From these persons, it was said, money and other presents were literally poured in upon him. But the day of reckoning came at last. Young says—

"Men may live fools, but fools they cannot die;"—

a beautiful dogmatism, but which, alas! has many exceptions, of which this man proved one. He lingered on for a time without much apparent change. That little was, however, downwards. Then he rapidly declined. One night he grew much worse. The following morning the nurse, after a short absence on her duties elsewhere, returned into his room, and—found him dead. He died "as the fool dieth." Some of the other patients on hearing of his death exclaimed "May the Lord have mercy on his soul." The precise nature of his illness was not clear to me. From what I could learn, it appeared to be a complication of disorders, a general breaking-up of the system, resulting from a dissipated and reckless life.

I will close this chapter with a serio-comic relation which I received from one of the officers of the institution.

The case occurred shortly before my admission. I give it as I received it.

> " I know not how the truth may be,
> " I tell the tale as 'twas told me."

However, from my knowledge of the party I received it from, I have no reason to doubt its truth. Strange characters are occasionally found as patients in hospitals; and strange things do occasionally happen in them, as elsewhere.—

Among the patients was a shabby-genteel man, of a stature invidiously called 'rather below the middle height.' He was a chemist and druggist's assistant or shopman. On the day following his admission a respectably attired female —I suppose I must say, a lady—called to see him, and was allowed to do so on her stating that she was his 'wife.' A short time afterwards a second lady called, and by a like statement to that made by the first one, also obtained admission. Then a third one came with like success. Each of these visitors not merely professed to be the 'lawful, wedded wife' of this Lothario, but was received by him in a manner that implied such a close relationship between them. Subsequently—I believe within three or four days—two or three other females called, each representing herself as either related or affianced to the unprincipled roué of humble life just referred to. After the departure of the second of the so-called wives, some remarks were whispered about that she did not resemble the one who had previously visited the patient; and on the visit of the third one it was at once suspected that some serious deception was being practised. Enquiries were made with very unsatisfactory results. It was evident that the man could have but *one* wife, and his being

15

married to even one of his visitors began to be doubted. Each lady, on being interrogated, re-affirmed her statement; and the gentleman (?) adroitly evaded direct answers to the questions put to him. The affair could not rest here; but what to do in it required consideration; and so some little time passed away. Whilst matters rested in this state it unfortunately, or, I should rather say fortunately, happened, that two of the females first alluded to met at the bedside of the man each of them called her husband. Bigamy and polygamy 'will out' as well as 'murder.' Each lady asserted her pretensions with equal vigour. Angry words came to blows; and the upshot of the matter was, that the ladies were shewn to the door of the building, and warned not to attempt to enter it again. The patient was now in an awkward predicament, and his state of embarrassment and confusion was absolutely ludicrous. On being directly charged with deception and infamous conduct in some shape or other, and having no means of avoiding an explanation, he cavalierly admitted his guilt in respect to three of the females, but said that he was a mere "gallant inamorato" of the others, and "did not intend to marry them!" The affair was now seen to be really a serious one. The Rev. —— —— was consulted; and during the day he lectured the profligate little druggist on the enormity and illegality of his conduct. In as short a time as the case would permit, the patient was discharged, and left the hospital followed by the contempt and sneers of every one. On reaching the doors he rapidly disappeared. What became of him subsequently—whether he escaped legal punishment, or figured in a police-court—was not known to my informant.

CHAPTER XIV.

My departure from the hospital—journey home—reception and scenes
there—incidents—relapse—convalescence—conclusion.

AND now the day arrived on which I had determined to leave the hospital. The usual preliminaries being gone through, I awaited the arrival of one of my family with a cab to take me away. It was my wish to leave early in the evening, to avoid attracting notice, as, with my head enveloped in bandages, I naturally should have done. Influenced by the same motive, I also wished to arrive home about eight o'clock; as I thus hoped to escape being disturbed by the visits of neighbours and friends to welcome me.

The nurse having arranged my bandages as firmly and artistically as possible, and in a manner which really did her great credit, I took my leave of the 'sister' and nurses, and such of the patients as I had become acquainted with, or from whom I had received acts of kindness. Then, assisted by my friend Mr. G——, one of the patients, to whom I have referred in the last chapter, and accompanied by my wife and eldest son, I tottered down the stone-steps of the large staircase, bidding adieu to others whom I knew on the way. The cab was waiting at the door, I was helped into it, and departed with my friends.

Notwithstanding my great desire to get home, I am in truth compelled to admit, that a weakness came over me now, and that I left the hospital with a temporary feeling of regret. I had been an inmate of it so long, had received so much kindness, civility, and attention, from every one connected with it, so many benefits from it, and had become so interested in all its concerns, and in its welfare and the welfare of those around me in it, that it would have been unnatural, and indeed, have evidenced ingratitude, had this feeling not come over me. On leaving the institution I received the congratulations and kind adieus of all I saw. They had my thanks and good wishes in return. May the blessings of God fall upon all of them in this world and the next, was, and still is, my humble prayer.

The night was a delightful one—the moon, near its full, shining serenely—the air remarkably clear, with not a breath of wind to disturb its stillness. The objects passed on my route—so familiar to me—seemed like old friends starting up to greet me; but nearly seven miles is a long journey for an invalid. Before I reached the end of it, the shaking and jolting of the cab gave me considerable annoyance, and I felt much exhausted.

At length my home was reached in safety—that home that only a few weeks before I feared I should never see again. How shall I describe my feelings on entering it? How shall I describe the quiet, earnest welcome that awaited me there? My feelings, for a time, nearly overcame me. I was helped to an easy-chair beside a roaring fire, into which I sunk nearly exhausted with fatigue. What followed from my family and friends, under such circumstances, may be anticipated by the reader; but there is one incident that occurred that I cannot resist relating. My faithful dog, that I referred to in an early chapter, met me at the gate, and evinced his delight at my return, but without his usual boisterous form of greeting. Then he ran before me into the house; and, when I was seated, took up a position at a little distance from me, where he remained, for a time, intently gazing at me. At last, quietly and unnoticed, he sprung upon a chair near me, and gently placing his fore-paws on my shoulder, licked my cheek. Then wagging his tail, and with every possible expression of contentment and delight, he came and laid at my feet. For several days afterwards when moving about the house, he did so noiselessly, and his voice was not heard; as if he feared he might disturb me. Greater part of his time he spent lying at my feet, or near me; or at my bedside or bedroom-door.[1]

After the fatigue of the journey home had passed off, I began to make a little progress, and this continued for some days. Then I had a short relapse. It came on one morning very early, after some hours spent in quiet sleep. I was suddenly awakened, and as suddenly compelled to assume the sitting posture in bed, by a fit of most fearful convulsive gasping, which lasted some time, and every moment seemed to threaten my dissolution. I never saw but one fit even approach it in severity; and that was in the case of a dying man. It ended in absolute exhaustion,

[1] This dog was one of the most sagacious, faithful, and affectionate creatures of his kind I ever met with. For a long time after my accident he spent much of his time daily in lying on the mat outside my study-door; every now and then snifting under it, or standing on his hind-legs trying to peep through the keyhole. When my torn and bloody clothes were carried home, he immediately recognised them, and whined piteously; and subsequently frequently resorted to the place where they were thrown, and again expressed his sorrow. Every night he kept watch, like a sentry, for my wife's return from the hospital, and minutely examined every article of my linen she brought with her. He was a beautiful animal, and had large, hazel eyes, as soft, lustrous, and expressive, as those of the gazelle.

followed by profound sleep or coma. By the time I awoke, a few hours afterwards, the state of my head and throat was again alarming, and many of the old symptoms had returned. Fortunately, by active measures and extraordinary care, I rallied in a few days; and in the course of eight or ten days returned to a similar state to that I was in before this last relapse. In another fortnight or three weeks I was able to walk in the garden, for a few minutes at a time, on each sunny morning; and gradually to increase the time until half an hour, and then an hour daily, was thus spent. And so I slowly, very slowly progressed; but it was not until nearly eight months later that the cold-water pads and dressings to my head and ear could be wholly dispensed with; and it was not until twelve months after the occurrence of my accident, that I could safely trust myself alone in the street. The very noise of wheels close to me threw me into such a state of trepidation that I lost all control over myself. Happily, though my illness and convalescence were long and tedious, they had a satisfactory termination; and, at the present time—though not so strong as before my accident, and still reminded of my injuries at every change of weather—though my mind may be occasionally depressed on my recollecting the losses which I have sustained, the "purposes broken off," and the trouble and inconvenience I have caused my friends—though some persons have taken advantage of my afflictions to wrong and persecute me—though another cloud has now crossed my path and thrown a gloom over my future life—I am otherwise in nearly as good physical health as I was before my accident.

And now, gentle reader, I must bring my narrative to a conclusion; but, before doing so, I have another revelation to make of, to me, a more afflictive character than any thing I have yet related. That dear being to whose noble devotion, and utter abnegation of self, I chiefly owe my recovery, is—

> ———————— "An angel now,
> "And treads the sapphire floors of paradise;
> "All darkness wiped from her refulgent brow—
> "Sin, sorrow, suffering, banished from her eyes."

*   *   *   *   *

The earthly form of one of the most gentle, amiable, pious, and unselfish beings that ever lived, to whom " doing good to others " was truly a labour of love, has departed from me. Yet I who was so 'near unto death'—I who am so tempest-worn and frail, am still here—still thinking —still existing—all but hoping. The day-dream of my fitful life is passed away. An 'enduring cloud' has fallen on me,—

> "And my soul from out that shadow shall be lifted—
> "Never more!"

APPENDIX.

ADDITIONAL NOTES.

Note to page 133.

[1] At the period to which this and the immediately connected chapters refer, my memory of current and recent matters of little importance almost entirely failed me. Thus I would enquire the name of a person perhaps a dozen times a day, and as often forget it. (See *p*. 44.) As a rule, recent occurrences were either for a time forgotten, or only obscurely remembered; whilst distant ones which had for years, often very many years, escaped my memory, again arose in my mind in all their original distinctness. The only present things that I permanently remembered were those that made a deep impression on me, or that deeply interested me; those of a subjective kind, doing so in the highest degree, were remembered best. It was thus with many of my visions and wanderings. The incidents of my childhood, even before I was three years old, frequently recurred to me with all their original vividness. In like manner the contents of books which I had read twenty, or even thirty years before, again came into my mind, and often, particularly with the poets, with such accuracy that I could repeat them word for word, and could hardly banish them from my thoughts. This supports the assertion in the Text, that "things are remembered in proportion to the strength and vividness of the first impression." It is thus that the aged generally well remember the events of their early days, but are oblivious of more recent ones. As soon as I began to mend, every thing that occurred before my accident, even some time before it, appeared to be of very recent date. And even during my convalescence this state continued, though in a less degree. Thus, unless I seriously reflected, I was apt to speak of seeing Mr. This or That

the "other day," or a "few weeks ago," although some months, or even two or three years, in some cases had elapsed since either of them. See *Note* to page 143; also *page* 236, infrà.

Note to page 139.

If my space permitted it, I could give numerous examples in support of the above views; and (D.V.) I shall endeavour to do so either in a future edition, or in a separate work on dreams, visions, apparitions, and delirium.

The occasional apparent 'fulfilment' of dreams, a point not referred to in the Text, seems to deserve a passing notice here. In such cases the vulgar and superstitious regard the dreams as of a supernatural character; but if they would take the trouble to investigate the matter, I think they would change their opinion. Either the event itself, or something connected with it, suggests the dream; or the waking thoughts of the party, probably fraught with anticipation, anxiety, desire, or dread, and continued or recalled in sleep, do so. In the first case the so-called 'fulfilment' *precedes* the dream, which it suggests through one or more of the senses, usually the ear; in the second case, it is mere accidental coincidence. The following, for the truth of which I can personally vouch, illustrate both cases:—

Mrs. H——, a respectable woman, resided with her family in a lone house on the banks of a deep, navigable canal, from which it was separated by a narrow carriage-road. One night she had a dream which much startled her, and which left such a strong impression on her mind, that though she slept after it, it caused her to rise earlier in the morning than usual. The substance of this dream, as related by her, is as follows:—"I dreamt I heard a man and woman talking together in the road near the end of our house. Presently the voices grew louder, and they appeared to be differing. I recognised the woman's voice as that of Mrs. —— (who kept a large shop in the adjacent town); and a few minutes after I felt convinced that the man's voice was that of her foreman. Then I heard the woman scream, and run away toward the drawbridge. The man chased her and caught her just after she had passed our house. I could now see them plainly. (It was a dark night, and the thick brick-wall of the house intervened.) High words ensued, and I heard the woman entreat the man to let her go quietly home. Then they struggled together. The foreman tried to abuse the person of his mistress, and then threw her into the canal, where, after two or three screams, and some struggling, she sunk. The man then ran away across the drawbridge toward ——. I heard —— church clock strike twelve just afterwards. When I perceived that the man was ill-using the woman I tried to scream for help, and to rise in bed, but could not do so. It was like one feels in nightmare."

This relation was at first received and laughed at as a dream, by all the dreamer's family but herself. By the next day, however, Mrs. ——'s dream got 'noised abroad,' and a few hours later an account of it reached the town. Enquiries were made, and it was then found that Mrs. ——, the shopkeeper, had been missing since early in the evening of the day on which the dream occurred. Next the fact oozed out that the foreman did not return home on that night until past one o'clock. Suspicions of foul play arose, and the canal was dragged. The body of the murdered woman was found close to the part pointed out by the dreamer. The state of her dress, &c., indicated that a severe struggle had taken place. Further investigation confirmed several other particulars in the dream. The foreman was arrested for the murder; but, unfortunately, owing to a slight defect in the evidence, of which he was given the benefit, he escaped the gallows. Subsequently a defective will was found which was evidently a forgery, in which the property of the murdered woman was left to the foreman.

In this case the event evidently preceded and suggested the dream. The dreamer's idea that she saw part of what she related, was, of course, purely imaginary.

The following illustrates the second class of so-called 'fulfilled' dreams:—

A near relative of the author's had extensive laboratories and a lofty pile of warehouses behind his dwelling-house, the two being separated by a broad paved court-yard. One of the top lofts was employed as a store-room for gunpowder and various fulminating compounds, of which an enormous quantity was always kept there. The wife of the proprietor had a great dread of gunpowder, and of the manufactures carried on in the laboratories. Indeed, the subject appeared to continually occupy her mind, and there was scarcely a night that she did not say on retiring to rest, that she "felt convinced that some time or other herself and family would be either blown up or burnt alive in their beds before morning." Soon afterwards her apprehensions of coming danger were greatly increased by the following circumstance:—A new 'hand' on the premises who had been sent to fill a bag with turnip-seed, unable to find the bin containing it, went into the powder-room, of which the key had been accidentally left in the door. Seeing two or three unheaded barrels of sporting-powder, he mistook it for the seed he was in search of. Thinking it looked "rather queer," as he expressed it, he took up a handful and proceeded down stairs to find the foreman or warehouse-man. Unable to find him, he crossed the court-yard and entered the private office of the proprietor in the dwelling-house. The proprietor immediately saw the man's mistake, and asked him 'where he had left his light.' He replied, "I stuck the candle in the middle of the barrel of seed whilst I came down here." My relative, for an instant, was 'dumfounded'; then he said "Stay here and mind my papers whilst I go and look at the seed myself." Then he went and cautiously approaching the barrel of gunpowder, placed his hands together so as to form a cup round the candle, and gently lifted it out. After securely locking the door, and removing the key, he returned to the man, and explained the circumstance to him, and the danger he had escaped. He next reprimanded the foreman, and issued rigorous orders for the safer conduct of this part of the business. From the warehouse the tale passed to the kitchen, and soon reached the ears of the lady through the servants. The following week she dreamt, on three different nights, that she heard the roar of fire; that she rushed to one of the windows of the bedroom, and on opening the shutters the panes of glass, intensely heated by the flames of the burning warehouses, cracked and flew in her face; and that the whole family escaped with difficulty in their night-clothes from the house, which, with the laboratories and warehouses, was burnt down. These dreams she related at the breakfast-table each morning after their occurrence. Now it strangely happened that about ten days afterwards her dreams were 'fulfilled' in every point except that the dwelling-house, though greatly damaged at the back by the fire, was not burnt down. The gunpowder, though damaged by the water from the engines, was removed by the soldiery before the fire reached that part of the building; a regiment of soldiers in barracks near the spot having turned out to assist in extinguishing the fire.

Here, I think, it is evident that the fears and anticipations of the waking thoughts were continued or recalled in sleep. The particulars that made up the dream were only such as were likely to occur if a fire took place, and would naturally arise in the mind of any one 'brooding' over the subject. Indeed there was nothing wonderful in such a person having such a dream. The event having shortly followed the dream was merely a case of coincidence. The same remarks apply to the more recent case of a woman who frequently dreamt that the powder-magazine near her house exploded and devastated the neighbourhood; an accident which subsequently occurred.

The dream through which the murder of Maria Martin at the Red Barn was said to have been discovered many years ago, as also of the spot where her body was buried, though very singular, may be explained, in the above way, without reference to supernatural agency.

Those who are interested in this and the other subjects noticed in this chapter would do well to read the following works, should they be able to obtain them. I did not myself meet with them until some time after the present work was written:—

"*On Hallucinations: a history and explanation of Apparitions, Visions, Dreams, Ecstasy, Magnetism, and Somnambulism.*" By A. Brierre de Boismont, M.D. Translated from the French by R. T. Hulme, F.L.S. London: Renshaw. 1859.

"*La Seconde Vie—Rêves et Rêveries—Visions et Cauchemars*" (The Second Life; Dreams and Reveries; Visions and Nightmares). Par X. M. Saintine. Hachette and Co. 1864.

Addition to Note, page 143.

My mind at this period was so full of the poets I had read and studied with delight in former years, particularly in early life, that frequently I almost thought in poetry, and poetical quotations linked together served me as the common language of my hidden thoughts and wanderings. Although I had not read through

"*Paradise Lost*" for a vast number of years, I could then repeat many of its 'books' correctly, though, when well, I could only remember the leading passages in them. Sometimes when I commenced deliberately to repeat one of these 'books' to myself, my mind, outstripping my mental recitation, would grasp sentence after sentence, with a rapidity so great that the whole was gone through before the former had embraced more than perhaps three or four pages; and yet during the whole time I had a perfect synchronal comprehension of each of them, although their matter differed. The same occurred with many of Shakespeare's plays, and with other works. This seems like double consciousness, as if the mind is dualistic in its action, if not in its existence.

Addition to Note, page 198.

And here I wish to say a few kind words respecting the nurses and 'sisters' of our hospitals. The first are often spoken of disparagingly by persons utterly unacquainted with their condition and duties. To constitute a *good nurse*, the party must be sober, active, industrious, good-tempered, and trustworthy. She must have some experience in her craft, be able to read and write, perform the minor surgical operations of dressing wounds, applying bandages, administering injections, &c., be able to pad and prepare splints, to assist the surgeons in their clinical duties, act in emergencies before the arrival of the surgeons, and do many other things besides mere domestic attendance on her patients. To possess these qualifications she must be a person who is above the 'ordinary run' of working people, or she must have undergone special training. Now it often happens that only *some* of the nurses in a hospital—perhaps only one in a large ward, or even in a set of wards—possess these qualifications; the others being commonly more or less inefficient, or more or less unsuited by their manners and habits for the office of nurse. How does this arise? I think it is referable to the very low salary paid such persons, the length and arduousness of their daily duties, and the drudgery which, apart from their attendance on the patients, they have to perform. The salary of an ordinary hospital-nurse, I believe, never exceeds £30 per annum, out of which she has to clothe and, for the most part, board herself; she is on duty generally at least fifteen hours a day; and she has, at intervals, to scrub the ward out (or pay for its being done), besides performing other drudgery. These things prevent a large number of respectable, well-qualified females accepting the office of hospital-nurse.

The usual salary of a 'matron' or 'sister' is, I am told, only from £36 to £40 per annum; a sum utterly inadequate to remunerate a respectable, efficient, and responsible female, for immuring herself in a hospital, and devoting her whole time to its duties.

A moderate increase of the salaries of these officials, and the removal of the drudgery now assigned the nurses, would, I think, not only be an act of justice, but also one that would tend to raise the character for respectability and efficiency of this portion of the working-staff of our hospitals. The welfare of the patients would undoubtedly be thus promoted, and in this, and other ways, the increased expenses would be more than compensated.

Addition to Note, page 199.

It must not be inferred from what is stated here and elsewhere in this book on the *dietary, &c.*, of our hospitals, that there is any extravagance and waste in them. Far from it. Every thing is conducted with the most rigid economy and care on the part of the governing officers; but nothing that is necessary to the welfare of the patients is denied them when ordered by the surgeons or physicians. This is a wise liberality; since through it many of the patients are rapidly restored to health or convalescence who would otherwise linger in the wards for weeks, or even months, without recovery, and, in many cases, succumb to the diseases or injuries from which they are suffering.

Note to page 226.

It will be seen from this and the preceding chapters that, although the greater number of the patients in our large metropolitan hospitals, as elsewhere, belong to the working and poorer classes, there are others there who belong to the middle and, sometimes, even to the superior classes of society. I was informed that during the twelvemonth immediately preceding the date of my accident, the brother of one of our most venerable and distinguished peers—a man of rank and wealth—was, for weeks, a patient in the hospital to which this book more particularly refers. His, I believe, was a medical case. The secretary of one of our

chief 'government boards' also lay there for several weeks following an accident that had befallen him. I could name other like instances. Persons of all classes, from all parts of the kingdom, also often repair to our great hospitals to undergo operations, or for the purpose of special treatment.

⁎ The liability to 'accidents' being common to all of us, irrespective of person or position, I think I shall serve the interests of my readers by enjoining 'preparedness' to meet them when they occur. This can only be obtained from a knowledge of "how to act" and "what to do" in emergencies of this kind. This knowledge is ably supplied in Dr. Schaible's inexpensive little work of which the *Title* is given below. From a personal knowledge of the subject, and from a careful examination of the book, I can conscientiously recommend it as one which I think should be in every household, and in the desk or carpet-bag of every traveller:—

"*First Help in Accidents : being a Surgical Guide, in the absence or before the arrival of medical assistance, for the use of the public, members of the military and naval services, volunteers and travellers, &c.*" By Charles H. Schaible, M.D., Ph. D., Royal Military Academy, Woolwich. LONDON: Hardwicke, 192, Piccadilly, 1864. 2s. 6d.

THE END.

www.ingramcontent.com/pod-product-compliance
Lightning Source LLC
Chambersburg PA
CBHW020756230426
43666CB00007B/716